Where Hippos Have Right of Way

True stories from nine years in the Okavango Delta

Sue Sainsbury

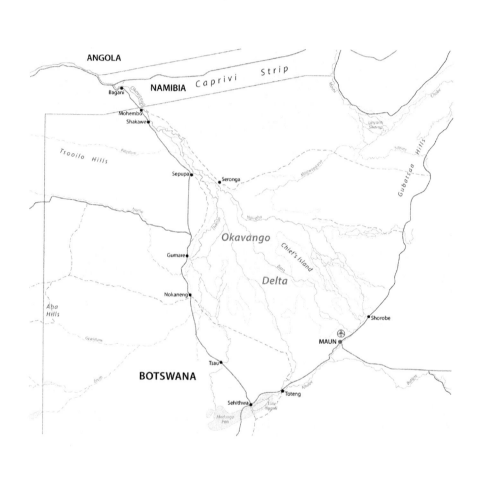

My mother died of lung cancer. I saw that she died with lots of regrets, things she was going to do and now never would. I vowed I would never be an old person who said "I wish I had ..." So I quit my amazing job, rented out my house and set off around the world.

I went to Botswana for two days and ended up staying nearly nine years.

Contents

Into the Delta

I arrived in Seronga in April 1998 to do a two day mokoro safari. On a small group overland trip from Cape Town to Vic Falls, we had stopped off at Ngepi Camp in the Caprivi Strip in Namibia where we camped overnight. Very early the next morning we were loaded onto open game viewing vehicles for the one and a half hour pre-dawn road transfer through the border to Sepopa Swamp Stop in Botswana.

From there we travelled by motor boat two hours down the beautiful Okavango River to Seronga. We zoomed along the river as the sun was rising and huddling together in the aluminium boat with a large outboard motor, we arrived severely chilled. Somehow I hadn't expected to be cold in Africa but night-time temperatures can drop to below zero in the Delta and speedboat trips can be quite cool even on a warm day.

After a quick briefing on arrival at Seronga we got into the fibreglass mekoro and headed out to camp on a remote island in the Delta. The first part of the trip was past houses and fields planted with maize. We saw grazing donkeys and cattle and families going about their everyday activities. Women tended their plants and cooked over open fires, young children washed clothes on the riverside – the real Africa.

Mekoro are traditionally made from the trunk of a sausage tree or ebony tree but when I arrived these were being replaced by fibreglass canoes. Geoff Randall from Guma Lagoon Fishing Camp had spent a long time perfecting the design and construction of the fibreglass canoes, based on traditional dugout canoes. The fibreglass canoes were lighter, straighter and more regularly shaped than the old wooden ones. This made them more buoyant and easier to steer and they also lasted a long time. There were fifty members of the Polers Trust that we were travelling with and if they all converted to using fibreglass canoes, that would save fifty mature trees from being cut down every few years.

I learnt that mokoro is the singular form and mekoro the plural. Mekoro are "poled" by men who stand upright in the rear of the mokoro and propel it by pushing a long wooden pole into the water, pushing off along the bottom. Travel is usually through channels made by hippos.

These channels can often be full of vegetation and the polers have to push hard to get through. It is hard work! Sometimes a big male hippo would decide that he didn't want anyone using "his" channel and he would rise out of the water as he heard a mokoro approaching, open his huge mouth and grunt warnings. Hippos always had right-of-way and sometimes the polers would have to spend days opening up new channels to avoid aggressive hippos before taking tourists out.

I remember one particular hippo who decided he didn't like motor boats in "his" part of the river. Boat drivers had to keep a sharp lookout for him rising out of the water in front of the motorboats; right on a sharp bend in the river. The boats travel fast and there were some very scary near misses!

Usually one or two guests from each group would try poling the mekoro and find that it certainly wasn't as easy as it looked. I found that I could pole or I could stand up but I couldn't do both at the same time. And it wasn't just about propelling the mokoro. Polers also had to know how to navigate, how to find the islands and how to avoid conflict with the animals.

Now, instead of avoiding interactions with elephants, lions, buffalo and hippos as they did in their daily lives, the polers had to actively seek them out to show their clients.

I will never forget the beauty and utter tranquillity of swishing through the water lilies in the open lagoons. I consciously took a "snapshot" memory that I knew I would recall when I returned to my normal stressful life.

As I lay in the mokoro leaning back on my backpack I felt such a sense of serenity. Down at water level in the mokoro I had a beautiful view of the pink and white water lilies with their vibrant green lily pads. The mokoro seemed to gently float through the perfectly clear water in this semi-open water and I was completely relaxed and at peace.

There was a guide leading the group – an old man called Sareqo Sakega who was to become like a father to me in Seronga. He obviously commanded a lot of respect from the other polers and when we reached the deserted island where we were to camp, he directed operations but didn't participate in the frantic setting up of the camp.

Tents were erected, latrines dug, firewood and water collected and cooking fires lit. Sareqo explained that we would have lunch and rest during the afternoon when the animals also rested and sheltered from the heat of the day. After our 4:30am start from Ngepi, we were happy to lie around under the trees in the shade.

In the afternoon we loaded back onto the mekoro and went off to see the hippos in a large, open pool about 10 minutes away. It was quite spooky to hear the grunting of the hippos who sounded as if they were right in front of us as their calls were carried across the still waters but they were actually a safe distance away in the large pool.

Our polers skilfully manoeuvred the mekoro to the edge of the pool, very aware of how close to get to these huge animals without threatening them. One large male took exception to one mokoro that edged a little too close to him and the poler beat a hasty retreat back into the shelter of the reeds – to the amusement of the other polers.

The next morning we were awoken early for a quick breakfast and a game walk. With one guide at the front of the group, and another at the rear, we travelled single file through the wavering long grass. This area is not a National Park – it is the real Botswana where people live alongside the animals. Mekoro are still used to travel between villages, for fishing, for collecting firewood and reeds for building and for transporting families and goods.

We had been briefed to stay quiet as we walked and warned that if we came across lions we should slowly move backwards, away from them. Running would have the same effect as rolling a ball in front of a kitten – we would be chased.

We saw a large herd of buffalo. If they had been individual bulls or small groups of males, we had been told that they might attack without warning. They do not mock attack and we should quickly find a tree to climb if we were chased. That made us quite wary.

The guides spotted a small herd of elephants amongst the trees long before we did. They dropped a small handful of sand to check the wind direction so we could avoid the elephants getting our scent too quickly. We circled closer and watched these huge animals calmly ripping bunches of leaves off the trees and feeding them into their mouths. We were soon noticed and the herd moved slowly away.

The polers joined us around the campfire that night and also sat and chatted with us during breaks. I discovered that we were the first paying group to go on safari from Seronga with Okavango Polers Trust. Some of the guides and polers had worked for safari companies in the past but for others this was their first chance to earn money. The Trust was started with the help of Willie Phillips and Anne Clift-Hill to allow the people of this area to have their own community-owned tourism business.

As we sat around the smoky wood fire under the clear starry sky of the African wilderness, I was so inspired by the genuine friendliness of the polers and their dream of working for themselves and improving their families and their villages. They told me that in three weeks' time they had to sit exams so they could get licences to work as polers or guides. Although they had the knowledge and experience of the area and the wildlife, many lacked Basic English skills. Part of the exam they were facing was to identify animals and sounds by their English names. I explained that I had one week of my trip left but that I would return and help them with English lessons until they did their exam.

After reaching Vic Falls in Zimbabwe I returned across two borders by bus and boat to Seronga. I was warmly welcomed back and Anne and Willie offered to let me stay in a small tent on their plot.

The polers had worked with Willie to clear some of the land to use as a camp and Willie had built an ablution block and established a reliable water supply. Willie's Camp was beside the river and when the flood was in, mekoro could leave straight from there. Travellers would camp overnight at Willie's Camp and then go on mekoro trips with the Okavango Polers Trust. Willie also had good relations with Audi Camp who were to provide the budget travellers and transport them to Seronga.

Seronga

Seronga is located at the bottom of the panhandle.From the air the Okavango Delta looks like a giant frying pan and the top thin part is known as the panhandle. Seronga is located where the Delta opens out from the panhandle.

It is the main village on the eastern side of the river, consisting largely of mud huts with thatched rooves but with an increasing number of concrete block buildings with tin rooves. The population numbers vary with many people coming and going but was estimated to be about 2,500. A lot of people leave the villages to work in towns or in safari camps in the Delta. In the past men would be recruited from here to work in the mines in South Africa.

The main tribe in our area was the Bayei. One person was a moyei and they spoke sayei.

Most people also have a "cattle post" where their cattle and goats are kept. They will often stay for extended periods at their cattle post or their fields where they grow maize, sorghum, beans, peanuts and watermelon. The fields are ploughed by cattle or donkeys after the first rains and then someone (usually the women and young children) must stay at the fields to weed and to protect the crops from baboons, monkeys and elephants.

Elephants are a huge problem in the area and it was sadly common to hear that the elephants had absolutely trampled someone's fields and eaten their crop just as they were ready to harvest. Fences don't keep the elephants out but there have been some successful experiments using chilli plants as hedges so this may become a solution in the future.

Even though the river is nearby and water is abundant, irrigation is almost never used. If the rains don't come, the crops fail. People eat well during the wet season and make do the rest of the year. With the river nearby fish is a significant part of the local diet.

Seronga had no electricity and limited running water. There were only a handful of telephones and no cell phone reception when I lived there.

In the middle of the village was the Co-op that sold basic groceries, a bottle store, a bakery, a bar and a shop located in two containers.

English lessons with the polers began with us gathered in a group in the campsite using a bird book, a wildlife identification book and photos I had taken on my travels. With these we could discuss the behaviour of all the animals as well as learning the English names. Classes were run every morning and afternoon and were well attended.

It was interesting to compare the facts in the books and known by some of the qualified guides with the many stories of animal behaviour from the older men. One example of this was when we were talking about hippos. The animal books told us that hippos go under water for about four minutes. This was vehemently denied by one of the old guides who insisted that when he had hunted hippos they could stay underwater for more than an hour. The younger more educated guides could have told him that the hippos had probably gone into the reeds and surfaced there but respect for their elders stopped them correcting him. We moved on.

One afternoon we were looking at the chapter on snakes and reptiles when the polers became excited and started yelling "Lebolobolo! Lebolobolo!" whilst pointing to the other side of the campsite. I then realised that they had seen a puff adder slithering across the sand in our direction.

A variety of birds also flew into the campsite every day, providing us with more teaching opportunities.

When looking at what animals are protected we had come to the section on snakes and were looking at pythons. Off to my side I heard "Ummm. They taste good". I quickly advised that they not mention that when they went to their exams.

One day after one of our English lessons under a tree in the campsite, I walked back into the village with a group of polers. As we walked I told them the English words for things and attempted the names in Setswana – much to their amusement.

Suddenly two donkeys thundered past us – one a fleeing female and one an obviously excited male. Right on the road in front of us, the male mounted the female. An awkward silence followed as O.C tried to decide whether he should comment or explain the Setswana term for this to this foreign woman they were still being excruciatingly polite to. We looked at each other, burst out laughing and then just kept walking as if nothing untoward had occurred. Indeed, it was to become a common sight and an acknowledged road hazard during the donkey "mating season". Donkeys with raging hormones are totally oblivious to anything else happening around them and cause many car accidents in the towns.

There were a lot of donkeys. Many had been purchased with cash compensation received after an outbreak of CBPP (Contagious Bovine Pleuropneumonia) in 1995 that resulted in the slaughter of 320,000 cattle in Ngamiland where Seronga was located.

The donkeys were used for riding and sometimes for ploughing fields but many were just valued as possessions but not used for much. They could often be seen wandering around the village with forelegs tied to another donkey so they couldn't wander too far or forelegs tied to each other to hobble the donkey and stop it straying. It was heart-breaking to see some tied with wire which had dug right into the flesh on their legs.

One day whilst walking to the camp I saw a poor donkey that had been attacked by hyenas. It was hobbled so it couldn't run away to escape the hyenas and they had bitten chunks out of it all over. It walked slowly along, dripping blood from all its wounds. I was so upset to see this poor animal suffering. I went to the Kgotla and begged the Customary Police to put it out of its misery but they said they couldn't do anything without permission from the owner. It was really frustrating. I believe it later died from its wounds.

The Okavango River enters Botswana from Namibia where it is known as the Covango River. As it travels down from the Okavango Delta, it spreads out to form the extensive floodplains. Much of the floodplains are covered with papyrus and reeds and from above look like solid ground. This vegetation is actually surrounded by water and is in some places so thick it is almost impenetrable. The islands that are there are thought to have originated from tree saplings growing on termite mounds.

Sitatunga are found in this part of the Delta. They are medium sized semi-aquatic antelopes which have adapted to living in the watery world. Their toes splay to allow them to spread their weight and balance on the water and floating vegetation. When startled, they run across the water and into cover. They can hide by submerging in deep water with just their nostrils above water.

Red Lechwe are also often sighted. Closely related to Waterbuck, they wade and can feed in water up to shoulder height but prefer shallow water. Although slow on land they can use their powerful hindlegs and elongated and splayed hooves to propel them quickly across water.

The bird life in the Delta is amazing – over 450 different species have been identified. The polers even knew where a rare Pel's Fishing Owl lived and this was a special treat for visiting bird-watchers. At any time birds such as the hoopoe, storks, egrets, hornbills, oxpeckers, weavers, doves, kingfishers, kites, buzzards, hawks, vultures and eagles can be seen. Not far from Seronga was a huge colony of Carmine Bee Eaters that nested in holes in the river bank.

Jacanas are interesting little brown and white birds that walk with ease across the water lily pads and other floating vegetation, using their long toes and long claws. They are good swimmers and can dive to catch aquatic insects to eat.

The female Jacana has a number of partners. She will mate with one partner and lay about four eggs in a nest he has made of partially submerged marshy vegetation. She then leaves her "husband" to hatch the eggs and look after the chicks while she flies off to find another mate. She will then leave him with the next lot of eggs and so on... If necessary, the males can carry the eggs under their wing and later, when startled, are often seen with little chick legs dangling from under their wings. The guides described the female Jacana as a bitch – someone who is not faithful, who sleeps around.

While sharing a campfire dinner with Ann and Willie, I reached for another piece of wood to put on the fire and felt something crawling up my bare calf. I instinctively reached down to flick it away and felt a sharp pain at the base of my thumb, followed by a horrendous burning ache. I had been stung by a scorpion. No sympathy from Willie as he pointed out that I should always check wood that I was picking up (easier said than done in the dark, although most sensible in hindsight).

My whole arm swelled up, right up to the shoulder. It throbbed painfully unless I held it up as though in a sling and it was almost impossible to sleep for the first two or three nights. The only treatment was anti-histamines and painkillers which I had to get from passing tourists as the village clinic recommended them but didn't actually have any.

The biggest problem I had was trying to look confident and uninjured as I helped to meet and greet groups of excited but generally nervous travellers who came to experience travelling by mokoro in the Okavango Delta. No sense in adding to their worry about harmful animals that might be encountered in Africa by explaining why I was nursing such a painful injury.

Exams

On the day before the Guide and Poler exams were to be held Willie generously drove his Scania truck with nearly thirty polers on the back all the way to Maun and I was invited to sit in the slightly more comfortable cabin with Willie and his dog. It was a long, hot journey along nearly 100 kilometres of sand road to the ferry crossing at Mohembo.

After careful manoeuvring to get on the ferry, we made it to the other side of the swiftly flowing river and then drove 400 kilometres on tarred road to Maun. Ann and Paul at Audi Camp provided very welcome food and accommodation and the next day the exams began. The polers were very nervous. Many had never even been to school and the idea of an exam was daunting. I found the Wildlife Department Officers very kind and helpful, making the polers more confident.

Then it was time for the long return trip by bus and boat as Willie had supplies to transport back to his shop so he needed his truck. By the time we got back to Seronga I really felt that I was part of this exciting venture and I knew that I could help. My background included teaching, small business management, travel and tourism – all skills needed to help the Trust get established and to work towards self-sufficiency. I was committed and decided to stay as long as I was needed.

After a few weeks Sareqo suggested I move into a home in his compound. Anne and Willie were busy building their prefab house which they had imported from South Africa and tensions were high around their camp. The polers were looking for their own camp site so they could become independent and avoid Willie's famous temper.

One of Sareqo's daughters had built the traditional round mud hut with thatched roof alongside other family huts but was away working at a safari camp and the house was available. I accepted gratefully.

The house was equipped with all the furniture and appliances a family could wish for – a double bed, a three piece lounge suite, a large coffee table, a wardrobe, a gas stove (with no gas) and numerous tables and other bits of furniture. It was hard to move around but so luxurious after my past months of living in a tent.

At around 5am on my first morning I was woken by a young child who had come to light the fire so I would have warm water to wash with when I got up. I sent her away with thanks.

When another child came later to do my washing I also sent her away with thanks. I then received a visit from Sareqo's wife trying to find out what the problem was. She explained that children should do my household tasks and when I again thanked her but explained that I would do all that myself, she walked away shaking her head at the strangeness of white people.

I was delighted when Ann and Paul from Audi gave me a solar outdoor shower which consisted of a black plastic bag with a small hose and plastic showerhead attached. The idea was to fill the bag with water each morning and then hang it all day in the sun. At the end of the day the water was hot. It worked perfectly and I was really excited to try it out.

Unfortunately, I soon realised that I was a great novelty in the village. As soon as the children realised that I was going to shower outdoors, they called all their friends and they all stood around to watch. I ended up "showering" in my swimsuit to the accompaniment of much laughing and commenting from about thirty children. I decided after that I would wash indoors using a tin bath like everyone else.

Sareqo had already built a two room home out of concrete blocks, with a tin roof. It was gratifying to see his standard of living visibly improving as the work he got through the Trust allowed him to buy glass to put in the window frames and when he had a real bed delivered from Maun. Most people slept on a thin mattress on the floor, all of the family in the one room.

All around the village people were improving their houses, starting small businesses and being able to buy things like school uniforms that they previously couldn't afford. In turn they were spending more money in the village.

Day to day life

Cooking was done outdoors over an open fire so my meals were kept very simple. Sometimes I could buy frozen chicken at the co-op or fresh fish from a local fisherman and even less often someone would slaughter a cow. They would string up the skinned carcass in a large tree in the village and word would go out that there was fresh meat. Unlike everyone else I liked lean meat – cuts like rump or topside. Batswana love their meat and know that gristle and bones add flavour. Being a fussy white person worked in my favour and I would often get a little bit extra thrown in as they didn't think I was getting the best cuts. Of course I had no fridge or freezer so anything bought had to be cooked and eaten immediately.

I learned to love rice (and more rice) and really enjoyed samp which was cracked maize cooked all day and eaten with beans. It was really quite tasty and I choose it whenever I could but didn't cook it myself as I was never home all day to look after it.

Vegetables were scarce but mostly consisted of butternut, cabbage and rape. Watermelons, maize, beans and sorghum were seasonal. I discovered things like chicken spice and rice spice that added flavour to tedious meals. I am sure they were probably full of msg but I didn't care. Tinned food also played a big part in my diet at that time.

I remember one occasion when I had returned home after a long day but before all of the polers had returned from their latest trip. I grabbed a book and went for a walk across the dry flood plain near my house. After about half an hour I selected a nice big tree and settled down under it to read my book and relax.

After not too long four polers turned up looking for their pay. Finding me not at home, they had simply followed my footprints and tracked me down. Hard to hide when you are working with seasoned trackers!

Each day I walked to Willie's Camp to meet tourists and to continue with training for the polers. Almost all had passed their Special Guides Licence which allowed them to take tourists in their mekoro. Six of the OPT members had renewed or gained their full Guides Licences. On our trips each group was led by a qualified Guide so these Guides were paid more and had more opportunities to earn money. They had to have good English so it was mostly the younger polers who became guides.

We were so lucky to have a good bakery in Seronga. Although they generally only made loaves of bread or sometimes bread rolls, every so often they would make donuts. I was always excited when I approached the bakery if I could see an open fire at the side of the building. A pot of oil would be put on the fire and when hot enough, the baker would drop dollops of donut mixture into it. They weren't the familiar round donuts with holes in the middle but they were sweet and they were fresh. Yum!

As part of our briefing when groups arrived we offered to stop at the bakery so they could buy fresh bread. It was another simple way of spreading the benefits of the Trust beyond those involved in the Camp and the Mekoro trips.

The one thing I didn't like about living in the village was the devil thorns. These hard, dry thorns have spikes on all sides and, wearing sandals, I was often stopping and pulling them out of my soft white feet. They really hurt and were designed to stay wedged so they could be distributed further. I consoled myself with the reminder that after the very first sign of rain, the thorns would sprout and send out long runners that supported beautiful yellow flowers. Overnight the village would be transformed with thick green creepers and yellow blossoms.

It never rained between April and November. And I mean never. You could leave anything outside with confidence that it wouldn't get wet.

October in Southern Africa was sometimes referred to as 'suicide month' as it was extremely humid and the heat was unrelenting. Small clouds would start to skid across the vast blue sky and we would look up repeatedly, hoping for rain. There were lots of thunderstorms and finally one would deliver the first rains.

The fat raindrops plopped onto the burning sand releasing a dusty smell. We sheltered when the rain bucketed down but then the storm would pass and we would carry on with whatever we were doing. No need for raincoats here.

We were lucky in Seronga because the floods reached us from Angola around March – about five months before they reached the other end of the Delta. And we always had the Okavango River. The sand and peat nature of the Delta acted as a natural filter and the water in the floodplains was good to drink.

Hippos and Pigs

One night I had to go to Willie's Camp as a group returning from the Delta had requested a traditional meal and dancing and I needed to be there to help organise.

I had been warned not to go near the floodplains at night but I was running late and thought I would be fine as this was a route I took at least twice a day.

I wandered along on my own in the dark with my torch lighting only a small area in front of me. As I went to duck through a bushy area to get back on to the road, I suddenly heard a grunt and saw a huge round shape in the bush in front of me. My heart beat fast with a surge of adrenaline. I quickly backed up and scooted off in the opposite direction. I was sure that I had disturbed a hippo – the most dangerous animal in Africa.

Hippos can grow to over 1500kgs and reach speeds of up to 30km/hour on land. They are very territorial and are often aggressive. They spend most of their days in the water keeping cool but move onto the land at dusk to graze on grass. I had been told that a hippo out of the water is often aggressive and that they hate having torches shone at them. What had I done?

Luckily for me it turned out that it wasn't a hippo but one of Sakuze's pigs. Mr Sakuze was well known in the area. Until he retired he was a Head Teacher at a Primary School and since his retirement had become very involved with local politics and was on the Board of the Okavango Community Trust. He had also played a big part in a written history of the Bayei language. He was often embarking on get rich schemes and apparently a few years earlier he had bought some pigs. They had proved difficult to contain and as pork wasn't really part of the local diet, it didn't look as though he was going to make much money from them so when they once again escaped from their pen he had left them to run wild.

They were still not the best animal to encounter in the dark but a lot safer than a hippo. I learnt my lesson and never walked down by the floodplain after dark again.

There is a great African legend about the hippo that goes something like this:

A long time ago the hippo lived on the land with most of the other animals. As he grew bigger and bigger his skin stretched and thinned. It was uncomfortable and the hippo got sunburnt easily.

He went to the creator and asked if he could move into the river. The creator told him "You will have to ask all the other animals that live on or in the river."

So the hippo gathered them all together and asked if he could move into the river. Some of the animals were concerned that because he was so big he might eat all of the fish. The hippo promised he wouldn't.

"If I am allowed to live in the river I will only eat grass and water plants."

"How do we know we can trust you?" they asked.

"During the day I will open my mouth wide so you can check that I am not eating fish. Every night I will come onto the land and spray my dung around so you check that I haven't eaten any fish – that there are no fish bones or scales in my dung"

The animals agreed to this and ever since, the hippo opens his mouth wide when he is in the water and sprays his dung on the riverbank every night.

Working together

Osimilwe Tshubelo – known as O.C. – began work with OPT as one of the coordinators. He had previous safari camp experience in Kasane and I found him conscientious and easy to work with. The coordinators were responsible for meeting and greeting guests and doing the pre-trip briefing. With good English, they were the link between the tourists, the polers and me. The coordinators prepared the work rosters and produced a report each month so all the members could see how many days each had worked. As mentioned, guides usually worked more days. They were the "Team Leaders" and were responsible for ensuring the safety and enjoyment of the guests. They were also paid a higher daily rate in recognition of their qualifications.

The coordinators were often in the firing line of complaints from polers who questioned the rosters and the number of days worked. O.C stood out for his organising skills and cheerful manner with visitors and locals alike. He became the Assistant Manager and I could trust him to do all that was needed whenever I was absent. We had a great working relationship and often had a laugh together.

Somewhere we had come across some old one thebe coins. They were no longer used because they were such a small denomination. These coins were actually small round pieces of aluminium. Ours didn't even have any writing on them. They were so flimsy that they bent easily and floated on water. It became an ongoing joke in the office that if anyone in the office did something good or finished a difficult task, we would give them one of these coins as a bonus. You never knew when they would turn up on your desk.

O.C lived in Gunotsoga and seemed able to avoid alignment with the Seronga or Xao groups.

G.B (Gabonomang Kgetho) was another of the coordinators. He had the most amazing huge smile and charmed all he met but he sometimes cut corners and bent the rules, resulting in him losing his job a couple of times but the Trust Board kept re-hiring him. At one time he formed a relationship with a German tourist who came on a mekoro trip and disappeared for about three months as he went travelling with her and even went to Germany for a holiday.

GB was also involved in a tragic accident. He was the driver on a motor boat that took some of the teachers out for a day on the river. The boat overturned and two of the teachers on board drowned. I am told that they simply sunk to the bottom and drowned. They couldn't swim and didn't shout or flail about or try to save themselves at all. It was almost as if they just accepted their fate.

It was a terrible time for GB who was put in a cell while the police investigated the accident. He was eventually released without charges.

Later, Kuze would work as coordinator. I wasn't sure how the men would react to a female coordinator but Kuze was very respectful and they accepted her decisions as she was always fair.

Tsogo was Sareqo's granddaughter. When the Trust began she was identified as someone to do the paperwork – maybe even be Manager but as the business grew and became more complex, Tsogo was happy to take on the role of Admin Assistant.

Kuze had worked in the office for quite a while and was organised and helpful. Her English was good and she stayed calm under pressure. I liked working with her.

She had some time off to have a baby and returned to work with the baby and a nanny so she could fit in breastfeeding breaks. All went well for a while until the nanny started using the Camp laundry to do all their washing and hung it all out alongside the road into the Camp. The baby was over six months old by this time and I suggested that the baby and nanny might have to stop coming to work with Kuze. She wasn't happy about this and left.

Rupes also worked as a coordinator. He was scrupulously fair and did a good job. Unfortunately one day when coming back from a buying trip in Maun he stopped off at a bar along the way and spent all of the Trust money that he had left over from the shopping. When he finally returned to Camp I insisted that the Board fire him. I felt he had abused the trust he had been given and also felt it had to be very clear that he didn't get any special treatment because of our relationship.

A couple of years later, after I had left, GB did the same thing and didn't lose his job.

Patrick was a qualified chef. He had worked at upmarket safari camps and it seemed he could cook anything. With Patrick in charge we could run the restaurant and offer catering at Mbiroba Camp. We catered a number of events for the Okavango Community Trust Board, for Conservation International and for 103 Skill Share workers.

The only problem I had with Patrick was that he was used to having a large staff under him and liked to give orders about prep and cleaning and then retire to rest. When I had to speak to him about this he got angry and demanded to meet with the Chairman of the Trust Board.

During this meeting he declared that he "didn't want to take orders from a white person". There wasn't a solution to this problem so we parted ways. Patrick went on to open his own little restaurant at his small village. His great skills were somewhat wasted as he cooked only traditional meals but he was back with family and working for himself so he was happy.

The polers' ages ranged from eighteen to eighty plus. I am not sure how people knew how old they were as birthdays weren't celebrated. In fact, when the Government decided that everyone should have an omang (ID card) I am told that many of the old people ran and hid in the bush. They were afraid that the Government might decide that there were too many old people and kill them off.

Where this idea came from I have no idea as it certainly wasn't based on any past event or the attitude of the Government. Botswana is, in fact, one of the more benevolent and democratic African countries and even has old age pensions. While not a large amount, these pensions provide the old people with some basics and luxuries like cigarettes, sugar and tobacco. Not having an omang made it very difficult for many old people to receive this pension.

One of our older polers was a small man – less than five feet tall with a very slim build – and he always wore a long, woollen army-type coat that hung down to meet his black leather work boots. He always looked as though he needed a shave and I don't think I ever saw him without his wide brimmed canvas hat tied on under his chin. He was always cheerful and although we could really only exchange greetings with my limited Setswana, I became quite fond of him.

His lack of sense of direction, limited strength and lack of English skills meant that he was always relegated to poling the luggage mokoro. Even then the younger polers would often take some of his load and help him when needed.

One year the Wildlife Service decided to come to Mbiroba Camp to test the polers for their licences. This saved the polers travelling all the way to Maun where they would have had to stay at least two nights. Peter Hancock and Frank arrived and were warmly welcomed by the polers who knew them from their visits to Maun.

One of the tasks the polers had to complete was to pole out from the shore, manoeuvre the mokoro in a figure eight and then pole back to shore. Sehembo provided great entertainment for all as he struggled to even pole in a straight line. He didn't get his Special Guide licence but as he never took passengers, he could still work.

Doctor was a lovely man. He must have been in his late 70s or early 80s and was short and slight but he was very fit and strong. One of my first memories of him was while we were waiting at the boat station for the latest group of tourists to arrive. With no phone and no radio at that time, we often had to wait all day if the groups were delayed so we would sit and chat.

That day I got one of the younger polers to translate and asked some of the older ones about their families. When we got to Doctor he announced that he had three wives but would be happy to make me his fourth. We all collapsed in laughter and Doctor was thereafter always referred to as my boyfriend.

I loved that so many people had aspirational names. In Botswana I met Doctor, Chairman, and Foreman. In Zimbabwe the names seemed to be more about virtues than occupations – Innocent, Precious, Praise, Honesty, Happiness. I would later work with Lovemore from Zimbabwe and met Promotion and Hope. I was also to meet a little boy called Saddam Hussein in Gudigwa where Saddam was regarded as a bit of a hero as he had opposed America. Many people identified with the challenges of blacks in America.

I realised just how much we are influenced by the slant given to news reports in our own countries. Colonel Muammar Gadaffi was regarded as a hero in Africa because he had so drastically improved the literacy and living conditions of his people and he even became Leader of the African Union in 2009. I heard that Nelson Mandela had a grandson named Gadaffi. I had always considered Gadaffi a ruthless dictator, guilty of genocide and horrific violence. Clearly I had heard different stories.

As time went on many of the polers adopted western names to make it easier for clients. Esekiel was tall, good looking, quiet and well spoken. He became Eric when he went on to become the Camp barman and took his job very seriously. He complained to me one day that people were helping themselves to the condoms which were left in a bowl on the bar "just for fun". I knew what he meant but couldn't help pointing out that maybe they were designed for fun.

While the polers were paid a daily wage, they depended on tips at the end of each trip to buy more than basic necessities. Our clients were mainly budget travellers so tips weren't excessive but an issue arose one day when the polers saw the clients giving tip money to their guide who was seen to pocket some of it and only pass the balance on to the polers. It was a hard issue to raise with the Guide without giving offence so I planned to handle it by suggesting that the clients tip the polers directly the next time he brought a group. This wasn't an ideal solution either as some clients would tip more than others. Polers with good English who interacted with clients more would also probably receive bigger tips. The tips were usually pooled and then divided evenly by our Guide. Luckily it was quite a while before the offending guide returned.

Mambo Mbambo was strong and hard working with a good knowledge of the area and wildlife but his English wasn't good enough for him to become a full guide. Mambo for some reason was known as King George and referred to as George by clients. He was darker skinned than many of our polers and when this came up in conversation one day the polers asked me why white people referred to themselves as white.

"You aren't really white. Some of you are orange coloured, some pink and some even have a purplish look."

"What colour am I?" I asked.

"You are orange" I was told.

I found Batswana were quite specific and literal about some things.

Fat and old is okay

I worked seven days a week, eleven months of the year and then in December I would head back to Australia to catch up with my family. I would return from my Christmas holiday obviously having eaten and drunk plenty over the festive season. On my return I would be greeted with "Oh, you are so fat!" As I became better known it was common to have this even called out across the street by people I didn't even recognise when I arrived in Maun.

Actually I wasn't fat at that stage in my life but clearly I was fatter than when I had left. I learned to smile graciously and thank them. I wasn't used to fat being a compliment but it is in this culture where being fat is a clear sign of being prosperous – having more than enough to eat.

I also had to get used to taking it as a compliment to be considered old. I was regarded as an elder in the village and was therefore treated with the respect given to elders. Although I was a woman I was allowed to sit with the men (on a chair) instead of on the ground with the women who were usually at some distance from the main event.

The polers called me Masadi Mogole which translates as old woman or grandmother. They assured me that it was a sign of respect. When I went to Maun I found that the other expats referred to me as Seronga Sue.

Men are served first at mealtimes, then women and lastly, the children have what is left. This can mean that the children don't get enough protein and I often saw young children with scaly patches on their scalp – I was told by a visiting Doctor that this can be a sign of protein deficiency.

It seemed that getting pregnant at a young age could actually be liberating for girls. Before they have children of their own girls are expected to cook, clean and look after younger brothers and sisters. Once they have children of their own someone else takes over these chores. There seems to be no social stigma attached to pregnancy out of wedlock and even stable couples may have two or more children before they decide to marry.

One weekend morning I walked along the river from my house to Willie's Camp passing by numerous young children (probably all under 10 years old) with tin baths full of washing. I felt a bit sorry for them. But on my return hours later I saw that the washing had all been done and clothes were draped to dry over low lying bushes along the riverbank. Some children were floating in the tin baths in the river, having a water fight. Others were climbing trees looking for Jackal berries or playing in the sand. It was reassuring to realise that children are still children and they made their own opportunities to play.

In the early days, bookings were done through Audi Camp. As we didn't have a phone O.C. or I would have to go once or twice a day to the co-op in the middle of the village and join the queue to use the public pay phone attached to the outer wall of the co-op building. If you forgot to ask something or mention something important, you would need to join the back of the queue and ring again. Arrival times were never exact and numbers often varied from those booked but the system worked – after a fashion.

One morning I awoke feeling really unwell – dizzy, nauseous and with an ache in my abdomen. I carried on, thinking it would pass but when I was on the phone to Audi I was hit by a wave of weakness and nausea, quickly ended the call and staggered into the co-op where they took one look at me and agreed to my request to use their toilet.

The workers at the co-op were very concerned about me and pushed me to go to the clinic. At the clinic I waited with about fifteen other people seated on hard wooden bench seats as I drifted in and out of semi-consciousness. The nurse diagnosed me as having malaria and brought me water and three anti-malaria tablets. I managed to get back to my house and collapsed onto the bed.

The next few days are very hazy in my memory but I remember Sareqo's family checking on me and trying to get me to eat.

Luckily I was seldom sick and never suffered an upset stomach or even a cold while I was in Seronga.

Rupes

The overland trucks usually had 20-28 clients plus guides and many times two trucks and/or a number of smaller groups would be arriving at the same time so we were able to provide lots of work for the local motor boats who did the river transfers between Sepopa and Seronga. We needed lots of boats to transport up to 70 people with their food and equipment.

Some people had used their compensation from the lung disease to buy motorboats and were able to make a living from doing these transfers.

One time we had organised eight boats to be waiting at the Sepopa Boat station to collect clients and we told them they had to wait until all the guests had arrived. One smallish group arrived early and demanded that they leave immediately. The boat drivers rightfully asked them to wait. So they went to the property next door - to 'Dupes' a South African who had his own boats and they asked him to deliver them.

On arrival he found me and demanded that I pay him. As we had already organised enough boats and we would still have to pay them all, I refused. I suggested he talk to the tour leader who had engaged his services. Dupes was angry and followed me around the village yelling at me.

The next morning he was still there so to avoid him I decided to go out to the Mekoro Station at Xao where we were dropping off a group and then waiting for another group to return. It was a lovely day for me – just relaxing and chatting to the polers and driver. One of these polers was Rupes – Maropamabi Maropamabi – who I found interesting and surprisingly charming.

While I was away Dupes went to the police and asked them to force me to pay. They agreed with me that we weren't liable to pay as I hadn't asked him to use his boats and he eventually went back to Sepopa.

Living in the village

The polers were keen to establish their independence and they regularly approached the Chief to ask for an office in town. Finally it was agreed that we could use one of the traditional mud houses with thatched roof that was located near the Kgotla (village meeting place). A reed dividing wall was built in the middle of the room and I moved into the back half with the front half to be used as an office.

I had enjoyed staying in Sareqo's compound but this was a temporary arrangement and his daughter would soon need her house back. We purchased and hung baskets on the reed wall to try to generate some income for other people in the village by reselling baskets to visiting tourists. I set up my half with a single mattress on the floor and a square mosquito net draped from the roof beams.

The first time it rained I realised that the roof leaked badly. There I was in the middle of the night, trying to get black garbage bags positioned over the mosquito net. It didn't work too well. All my bedding was wet and I didn't get much sleep. The garbage bags had to become a regular feature of my bed during the wet season.

Our next move was to another building owned by the Kgotla. This one was opposite the bar and was built of concrete blocks with a tin roof. There were two rooms so I set up one as my bedroom and during the day I would push the mattress up against the wall and the room became our classroom. The second room was used as an office and contained two old wooden desks and a few chairs. We had some tourism posters that featured Botswana wildlife and whenever we obtained photos, we would put them up as well. We purchased a big, old fashioned safe and eventually a gas operated fridge so we could sell soft drinks.

This building didn't leak but with a tin roof it could become unbearably hot. Of course we had no electricity so we couldn't even have a fan. I have vivid memories of sitting at my desk just before the rains came doing paperwork with the chair pulled out from the desk and my head angled down so the constant stream of sweat would drop onto the floor – not onto the papers.

My first February in Seronga I was invited to the Police Christmas Party. I know, most people have Christmas parties in December. This one was long promised but slow to organise.

In the village there were two sorts of police. The Botswana Police dealt with criminal matters and in Seronga were responsible for the river and waterways as well.

The Traditional Police dealt with civil matters and worked with the Kgosi (Chief) at the Kgotla (meeting place). All of these policemen came from other areas and this allowed them to be impartial when dealing with local matters.

The Police Station was a small concrete building located near the Boat Station and the policemen lived in small basic houses out the back. Behind their houses was an open paddock and the party was held there in front of a huge bonfire. On arrival we bought a card of tickets which could be exchanged for beer or food. There was good music and good company and my path crossed with Rupes again.

I began to spend more time with Rupes over the next few weeks and after I moved into his cousin Moeletsi's house he eventually moved in with me. We began an on-again, off-again relationship.

We were both stubborn and Rupes was very proud – quick to take offence. I, on the other hand, probably wanted more priority in his life than a Motswana man likes to give. Despite all of this we had a lot of fun and my time in Botswana was much enriched by Rupes' input. He would quietly give me backgrounds on people we met and advised me on how to behave appropriately. Spending time with his family in Seronga and in Maun meant a lot to me.

The grass airstrip was about halfway between the office and Willie's Camp – probably a kilometre walk. I thought it would be a good idea to use a donkey cart to meet people off the planes and boats and transport their luggage to the campsite and mekoro. I had seen plenty of donkeys around and a few people owned donkey carts so we started asking around. Prices to buy these were unrealistic so we decided to hire them. I hadn't realised how complicated this was going to be.

I found that I would have to hire someone to round up the donkeys every day and then I discovered that unless you hit the donkeys on the rump with a long stick, they often wouldn't move at all.

On the way to the airfield the donkeys would move slowly with the "donkey boy" running alongside them hitting them. On the way back the donkeys would realise that they were headed home and they would take off! Not the image we wanted to portray to visitors.

This venture didn't last long but years later Donkey Boy was still known in the village as Donkey Boy.

The only bar in town sat in the middle of the village on the corner opposite Anne and Willie's container shop and was called the Overseas Liquor Restaurant. I am sure visitors thought this had some reference to overseas visitors but in fact it was thus named because everyone referred to the settlements and villages on our side of the river as "overseas".

It was a Liquor Restaurant rather than a bar because its licence required food to be served. This happened from time to time when wood-fired BBQs cooked meat on grates balanced on top of half 44 gallon drums. Occasionally chips were also available in the bar. Mostly it was a gathering place for those who had enough money to buy beer and a meeting place to "hook up" for the night.

Before we had Mbiroba Camp we would take tourists there to experience some local "culture". My abiding memory is of noise and excitement and the persistent beat of reggae music. Buffalo Soldier was a particular favourite that was played often and loudly.

Tourists were often hassled to buy drinks for the regulars but I think this was accepted as the currency to mix with the locals. We usually tried to be around to make sure no-one went too far and to remind our visitors that it wasn't respectful to walk around shirtless and it was against the law to walk back to camp with open cans of beer. Such visits provided a good boost to the income of the local bar owner of course.

The Overseas Liquor Restaurant sold commercial beer brands such as St Louis and Lion but these were considered expensive. Local beer, on the other hand, is very cheap. Called khadi, it is made of berries and sugar. It is made in the morning and drunk in the afternoon. It is usually made by women who sell it in their yards. I found that it tastes like fruit juice or apple cider but has a hidden punch. Sometimes it is so strong it makes the lips and mouth completely numb. Its' biggest danger is that its alcohol content can vary enormously. I heard stories of people being blinded by alcohol poisoning after drinking khadi.

Matilda

Our tourist numbers were picking up and the water level was dropping after the flood so it was getting difficult to pole the mekoro from Willie's Camp out into the Delta. Audi Camp offered to bring a vehicle and driver to help transport guests to the permanent water out near Xao. Ann Uren arrived one day with Matilda.

Ann and Paul had named all of their vehicles and Matilda was a wonderful old land cruiser. A South African friend of Ann's son came and the plan was that he would stay and drive Matilda. A large group had just returned from the Delta and gathered in the Overseas Liquor Restaurant. Our new driver joined them and when he returned announced that there was going to be a party at Willie's Camp that night where the group was overnighting before continuing their trip. Ann made it really clear to him that he could go but he wasn't to take Matilda.

Ann was staying with me in Sareqo's house and we were surprised to hear Matilda start up about an hour later and drive off towards Willie's Camp. Ann was furious and we walked the two kilometres to Willie's Camp where she tore a strip off the young man and informed him that he was on the plane home the next day. Thus I became the driver.

I didn't want to point out that I had never driven a four wheel drive before and I certainly had no experience driving in soft sand. A quick lesson from Ann and I was on my own. I got stuck a couple of times but mostly because of the ritual of locking in the wheel nuts for four wheel drive. I was usually with others and they would jump out and lock or unlock the nuts. Unfortunately sometimes the nuts would be unlocked when we needed four wheel drive because they had been already locked.

Later when we had our own Land cruiser I got stuck in the middle of the village. I had been driving around letting cooks and traditional dancers know that they were needed the next day as all the other staff had left to attend Church. I had to drive off the usual tracks to get closer to their home compounds and I struck a deep pocket of soft sand and just couldn't move.

I thought that the hubs were already locked in as one of the polers had earlier jumped out and "locked" them for me. What I didn't know was that the hubs had already been locked and my helper had actually unlocked them. On my own by this time, I got very hot and bothered trying to get out of the sand and eventually left the vehicle where it was and walked home hot, sweaty and frustrated. I was very embarrassed the next day when I went back with the driver who simply locked the hubs and drove off!

Matilda was strong and steady and served us really well until we got our own vehicles. We had no real mechanics in the village but there were a number of "bush mechanics" who had some experience and managed to keep us going. Also, if Willie was in a good mood he could help us fix anything.

Snakes and Chameleons

One day we visited Rupes' aunty in Maun and she gave me a young hen. She had the most enormous hens I had ever seen and it was quite an honour to be given one. But Maun is five hundred kilometres from Seronga and there I was with my chicken to take home. It wasn't unusual for people to travel with chickens but it was a new experience for me.

Once I got it home I realised that it would be lonely on its own so I mentioned that I would like to buy some more. Children started arriving at the office with a chicken under their arm. Eventually once I had five chickens I had to let people know that I had enough.

All around the village I had seen the traditional chicken houses I really loved the traditional chicken houses which were little pointy thatched houses mounted on a platform and reached by a narrow ladder. I organised a couple of young guys to build me one. I thought it was wonderful but my hens wouldn't come home to sleep there. Each night some of the children who lived nearby would bring my hens' home and put them in their house until they learnt where they lived.

One night I drove home in the Trust's land cruiser and as I parked outside my house the headlights lit up the chicken house and all I could see was a very long snake with its head inside the chicken house and its body stretching right down to the ground. I decided to drive back out and fetch Simon, a white friend of Willie's who had not long moved into the village.

Although pythons are protected in Botswana I knew that if I went to my neighbours for help, they would kill it. It had committed the unforgivable sin of interfering with domestic animals and the locals had a habit of killing all snakes they saw anyway – just in case they were poisonous. I also knew that python is considered particularly tasty.

I arrived back with Simon, armed only with a long stick to pull the python out of the chicken house. Simon took one look and insisted we go back to his place for a gun. It was actually a deadly cobra. The two chickens that survived the attack died the next day so I decided not to replace them.

I took the body of the snake (over 2 metres long) back to the office and put it in the freezer part of our gas fridge, thinking what a great teaching aid it would be. Unfortunately, even though it was obviously dead and frozen, none of the polers would come near it and insisted I get rid of it. We skinned it and I had the skin in my office for quite a while but it was always regarded with great suspicion and one day it disappeared.

I had a similar problem when I found a semi-hibernating chameleon.

At that stage we had only a few reference books to use in classes and I thought it would be really interesting to have a live chameleon to look at and discuss. I had it in an old shoebox and when I opened the box and the polers saw what was in there, they literally stood up and ran out of the room. I hadn't realised that chameleons are regarded as extremely unlucky and are killed on sight.

Even when it was back in the box, my students wouldn't come into the room. I was living in the middle of the village and the problem I had was trying to let it go somewhere that it wouldn't be immediately spotted and killed. I waited until it was dark and crept out and put it on a tree. I never saw it again and tell myself it went off and had a long, healthy life.

I was told off by Rupes one day when we were driving home from Maun and I swerved to avoid hitting a chameleon walking slowly and cautiously across the tarred road. He could not understand why I would bother.

Our own camp

The Trust members really wanted their own campsite and over time we managed to be allocated land about four kilometres out of Seronga. We could now apply for funding to build the Camp.

Botswana has some wonderful funding opportunities for citizens and community enterprises and I moved to Maun for a week, borrowed a friend's computer and filled out funding applications. I could research some costs but I have to admit that I just guessed others.

We did amazingly well. We received significant grants from the Government funded FAP (Financial Assistance Policy) and CEDA (Citizen Entrepreneurial Development Agency). We also received a grant from ADF (African Development Foundation) which made possible the initial development of the campsite. The wonderful staff from this organisation became our treasured advisors and supporters. A grant from the European Union enabled us to purchase the truck and provide training for polers, staff members and local community members.

All of this funding enabled us to build the Camp, buy a motorboat, a land cruiser, and a Samil truck. We were also able to provide a lot of training.

For the first four years of operating the Camp we received subsidised wages. The first year we received back 80% of all wages paid to citizens, the second year 60%, the third year 40%, and the fourth year 20%. This meant that we could employ a lot of people. As well as the 75 members of the Trust we employed housekeeping staff, kitchen staff, cleaners, gardeners, security staff, drivers and office staff. The Trust was now supporting about a hundred families directly and the wider community indirectly. I tried to help the Trust members understand that this was an artificial situation with an end date. We had many discussions about the need to retain some funds to run the business and to make provision for future maintenance and development. Unfortunately I never succeeded in changing the ingrained attitude that all income from mekoro trips should go to the polers. They really couldn't accept that all the other costs of running the business had to eventually be covered by what we were paid by the tourists.

Later we received some funding from The Canada Fund to allow us to purchase radios and First Aid kits and to provide some First Aid training. We could now communicate with the vehicles and to the mekoro station at Xao. Every group that went into the Delta now took a radio and First Aid kit with them. It would still be a long trip back to get help in case of an accident but we felt that it was now safer and our operation was more professional.

After long discussions about the name of the camp, the Trust members decided on Mbiroba. There were many interpretations of the meaning of the name, depending on which language it was attributed to. Finally it was agreed that Mbiroba meant Bush Camp in the River Bushman or Bukakhwe language.

The Board members worked with a Maun-based English photographer Stuart Arnold to design and produce a smart, glossy brochure and a website.

Once the campsite was cleared we were able to book groups in there to stay overnight. Long-drop toilets and bucket showers were constructed. George was employed as caretaker and he was supposed to be at the Camp every night – even when there were no guests.

We knew he didn't do this. He lived near the camp and if we ever went there after dark he would hear the vehicle passing his plot and hastily rush through the bush to arrive sweating and panting just after we got there. Of course he denied doing this.
Part of his job was to collect wood and light fires for the guests

and to heat water for the bucket showers. These showers were quite effective. A metal bucket with a shower head attached on the bottom was filled with warm water, hoisted by pulley over the person waiting in the shower area who would open the tap and have a warm shower.

Later a plumber from Maun was employed to build storage tanks and put in water pipes so we could have running water and flushing toilets. For some people in the village these toilets were the first they had seen and great interest was shown in how they worked.

We wanted to tile splashbacks on all the basins in the ablutions blocks and chalets but none of us had done any tiling. Luckily a passing tourist told us he knew what to do so after a quick lesson from him, O.C. and I were now tilers.

Solar panels and batteries allowed us to use a computer. However, the phones and internet were quite unreliable and internet charges were based on time used – not data downloaded so it was really frustrating to wait for connection and then have to give up and try again.

When we had obtained funding to build the camp and we explored how we wanted it to look. Some of the Board Members had experience working at other safari camps in the Delta and they were keen to have their camp look like these. I tried to guide them to understand that we were catering for budget travellers, most of whom would prefer to camp and would have their own equipment. Our clients weren't the low volume / high income tourism favoured by the Botswana Government but our model provided more employment, especially to less educated villagers who could make use of their amazing knowledge of the environment. It was cultural tourism without the artificiality of traditional villages set up only for tourists.

After a number of discussions we went out to the site. All of the undergrowth and many of the smaller trees had been cleared and in this dry season there was a lot of sand but also some beautiful old trees; in particular a spectacular sausage tree. The sausage tree can grow to 20 metres tall and provides beautiful spreading branches that just invite you to camp under them.

Unfortunately the sausages that give it its name can grow to weigh up to 20kgs. Having one of these sausages land on you could be fatal! The flowers of the sausage tree grow as pendulous purple/red fronds that don't smell great to us but certainly attract the bats and insects that pollinate them. When they drop on the ground they provide a beautiful colourful blanket under the tree.

The Board and I spent over an hour walking around the site and discussing where the bar and restaurant should be located, where the chalets and ablution blocks would go. Although it was tempting to locate the bar down on the river at the bottom of the site, I thought the Board members understood that with the bar located so close to the town and owned by the local villagers, it would be used by visitors from the village so it was best to put it near the entrance and away from the campers. The best sites were to be reserved for the campers.

We went back to the office and started to draw up the site plan. It soon became clear that every Board Member had a different idea about what we had agreed on. Eventually we reached agreement, the plans were drawn up by a South African architect and I went home for Christmas.

When I arrived back a month later I found that the half built bar was at the river and facing uphill – away from the river. In my absence, the Board had decided it would look better at the river and regrettably the builder had flipped the plans and the building was back to front. We reached an expensive compromise where we paid half and the builder paid half to put it back where it needed to be.

Although OPT started in Seronga and was based in Seronga, it was open to all polers who lived between Seronga and Gudigwa.

When trips started from Willie's Camp it was a simple transfer on foot from the motor boats or airstrip to the camp. When the floods started to recede the trip from Seronga by mokoro became almost impossible. The mekoro dragged over the vegetation covered by only inches of water. This was really hard work for the polers and not very interesting for the guests as it started to take longer and longer to get out into the parts of the Delta where the water flowed freely and wildlife abounded.

So it was decided to establish a mekoro base at Xao – about twenty minutes by road from Seronga. A significant group of the members came from this area and they agitated to have the Trust based in Xao. This wasn't practical once the land was allocated for Mbiroba Camp near Seronga and the suggestion to move hadn't been well received by the Seronga polers who had started the Trust.

Building Mbiroba Camp

It was a cause for great celebration when we were finally allocated land outside Seronga Village.

Our first job was to build a road through the bush so we could start clearing the campsite. Ramasimo was one of our older polers and had apparently had some experience so he was put in charge of this job. Ramasimo was a quiet, extremely hardworking man and he set to work quickly with his group of labourers. Unfortunately the huge road he built, which would seriously have made a good highway, was right through someone else's land.

We didn't realise this until we were visited by an irate lady who said the land had been left to her many years before. She had never cleared the land or used it so our workers were unaware of her ownership. With apologies we started again, pointing out that she now had land cleared ready for planting so no harm was done. The new road was less direct, much longer and more a track than a highway after we reined in Ramasimo's enthusiasm a little.

Each year we would attach a large truck tyre to the land cruiser with chains and drive up and down the road dragging the tyre through the sand to flatten out the bumps and holes that developed during the wet season. We also needed to cut back the scratchy thorn trees regularly.

After getting our Camp plans drawn up by the architect we asked around and sourced a builder who had experience in building upmarket safari camps. In addition to the bar/restaurant, reception, a Manager's house, the Polers Meeting Room, a garage area, and two ablution blocks, we were to build five two storey chalets.

The builder decided that the chalets were over-engineered and needed only one big beam to run the length of the building – not the two on the plans. The rooves were very steep and thatched and carried a huge weight. The builder assured us that removing the extra beam was the way to go.

The building of the chalets was nearly completed when we arrived at work one morning to discover that one of the chalets had folded up like a pack of cards during the night. The next day we were all in the office when we heard a huge cracking noise and then a loud thud. Another chalet had collapsed. We were just grateful that no-one was working in the chalets at the time. The builder had to fix all of the chalets.

To spread the prosperity around the village we had decided that the contractor would assemble the pole structure, the wooden staircase and the thatched roof and we would get five different local builders to do the rest of the building work – a different one for each chalet. Part of the walls would be made of reeds as this would give employment and income to many more community members and make sure that the Trust could do its own maintenance in the future. A large group of women collected the reeds, boat drivers made money transporting the reeds and a group of women assembled the walls, weaving the long reeds together with creosote soaked string.

While the building work was happening I would arrive at the Camp each day and O.C. and I would visit all the builders and see how they were going. They all had the same set of plans but every day we would have to ask questions like "Why is that window there?" and "Shouldn't the door be on the other side?" Still, we got there in the end and gave work to so many people in our area who then had a greater sense of ownership of the Camp than they would have had otherwise.

When the chalets were finished lots of people walked from the village to see them. One group of older ladies came because they had never seen a staircase. The wooden staircase was open so you could see through the gaps between the steps. They went up the stairs a little nervously and we had to encourage them to come down. They regarded the wooden stairs with great suspicion then they had a little discussion and all three sat down and came down step by step on their bottoms.

It was too expensive to import bricks into Seronga. Often the sand road from the ferry was so bad that only the bravest truck driver would attempt driving the one hundred kilometres from the ferry. There were also restrictions on the weight of trucks allowed on the ferry. So we decided we would have to make our own bricks.

We imported the cement from Maun a few bags at a time and hired a couple of brick moulds from people in the village. Suitable sand was available on the other side of the village and we had our Samil truck by then so sand trips were organised whenever the truck wasn't needed for the guests.

Our driver, Molete, would set off with a dozen or more strong men and shovels and collect a truck load of sand. The sand was located down quite a steep slope and one day I was called to the radio because Molete had called to say he was stuck halfway up the slope and couldn't get to the top. After checking that he hadn't overloaded the truck with sand, we finally realised that the heavy load plus the twenty helpers were just too much! Molete unloaded all the people and managed to reach the road.

We levelled an area just outside the campsite on the riverbank so the bricks could be made and dried. This gave work to another ten or so people for months. It became a popular area for the elephants to gather and sometimes I would sneak out of the office and go to the riverbank to watch the elephants. If there were tourists around one of the workers would come up to the office and tell me that "our cattle" are back. We would quietly go off to watch the elephants who wandered all over the site and never once trod on or knocked over the rows of drying bricks which were tightly packed in rows.

We decided to build five round thatched rooms (rondavels) in case they were needed for staff accommodation and furnished them each with two single beds. Being so close to Seronga, staff accommodation wasn't really needed and these buildings became budget accommodation.

Furniture, fridges, freezers etc for the camp were all purchased in Francistown. Rupes and I would drive the 1000kms there in the land cruiser, visit Telekoms, the Lawyer, Government Departments and then shop at Game (a discount department store). We always returned to Seronga with the land cruiser fully loaded and also organised delivery trucks for what we couldn't fit. Some things such as restaurant equipment were bought from South Africa. We had material for bedspreads and curtains custom made in Zimbabwe for the chalets. They featured hippos, elephants and giraffes. I started making the curtains myself but was then delighted to find a lady from a nearby village who had trained as a dressmaker and she took over – another person getting employment through this project.

The Manager's House felt like absolute luxury to me. It had two bedrooms, a small kitchen and a real bathroom with a flushing toilet and a shower with hot and cold water. Its steel-framed windows were covered by curtains using African themed material from Zimbabwe, similar to what we had in the chalets. The house was surrounded by a reed wall which gave it privacy.

I tried to establish a vegetable garden in the area behind my house but it wasn't very successful. The sand was very fertile but it was just too hot. Plants shot up and went straight to seed.

To thatch the rooves of the rondavels we had to organise our own thatch and thatchers. Most safari companies bought their thatch in South Africa. We bought what we could locally but after investigating the options we decided to get ours from Namibia which was only 120kms away.

We made a trip across the border to find suppliers and arranged for them to deliver to us in Seronga. We then had to find thatchers and of course someone knew someone who did thatching. Thus we met J.J, Louis and their gang of workers who had actually worked on the chalets. They turned out to be a great asset. Not only did they quickly complete the thatching at a reasonable price, but they also helped with lots of other building jobs around the Camp.

The building company we had contracted had built the large thatched roof to house the bar and restaurant with a concrete floor and supporting poles but no internal walls. So it was up to us to decide where walls would go, how big rooms were etc. J.J and Louis had experience at other camps and provided a good sounding board for our ideas.

We put two toilets near the bar and I was called in front of the Board to explain why I would put a smelly toilet so near to food. I had to explain that we were installing flushing toilets not long drops.

I asked the guys if they could build swinging bar doors like you would see in a Western movie. Another cultural reference that meant nothing to them! But following my amateurish drawings, they understood what I wanted and built beautiful wooden swinging doors. They also made fittings such as toilet roll holders and towel rails out of small branches for all the camp.

We installed solar panels and batteries to provide lighting and enough electricity to run the computer and radio at the Camp – as long as we didn't use it too much.

Each chalet had a solar panel and battery and these were inspected and cleaned regularly. One day it was discovered that one battery was missing. After asking around we found that one of the guides had taken it home 'because it wasn't being used'. He was happy to return it when asked and didn't think he had done anything wrong.

Once the bush was cleared in the campsite we had only dry sand left. We spent many hours collecting grass runners from the riverside and replanting them in the campsite. By putting in irrigation and sprinklers, we were able to keep the grass alive but the water pressure wasn't good.

We also bought a large number of bougainvillea plants which we positioned along the perimeter fence near the restaurant. The colourful pink and orange flowers made great decoration for the tables in the restaurant and looked nice growing along the fence.

Busy Times

Getting a phone to the Camp was a priority. There were some phone lines in the village but they ended over two kilometres from the Camp. On every trip to Maun I would visit Telekom and try to pressure them to extend the lines to us. I wrote many letters and also visited Telekom in Francistown and politely begged them to help us. I kept up my persistent barrage of requests, emphasising that this was a community business that was benefitting the whole community.

One day a work crew turned up at the Camp and their supervisor informed me that he had been told "to make that woman happy" and negotiations began. He argued that they couldn't do the installation for free as other safari companies would complain about unfair bias. I was told that it would cost 117,000 pula to put in the new poles and lines.We didn't have that much money but we finally agreed that the Trust would pay the 12,000 pula that I had originally budgeted for and work began. Once we had the phone lines we could also get internet (unreliable as it was) and we could take direct bookings.

Phil and Kay Potter from Island Safaris arrived to meet with the Trust. I was impressed by the respect they showed to the Board with Phil and the other men changing into long pants and Kay into a skirt before the meeting. They patiently negotiated to bring their own clients to Seronga, using their own boats and Sepopa Swamp Stop. They would later buy Swamp Stop.

The Trust business boomed. In one year we had over four thousand eight hundred visitors. This gave work to all of our members and to lots of casuals as well. Sometimes we were so busy that as polers returned from a trip, we would meet them at the mekoro, give them more provisions and they would head off with a new group for another two or three days.

If we were short of polers (even after we increased the members from 50 to 75) we would drive around the village and pick up anyone who could pole. I was amused when we would stop and recruit someone who might be on the way from the fields or from collecting building materials and I would ask if they wanted us to send a message to their wife/wives explaining where they had gone. O.C had to explain to me that it was not up to a woman to ask where her man was or had been. Another cultural difference I had to learn.

When I first learned that most men had more than one "wife" I assumed that jealousy mustn't be an issue. How wrong I was! During my time in Seronga I heard of many jealousy-fuelled fights and even killings or suicides.

It was explained to me that often a man would have a wife who was pregnant. With about three months to go before the birth she would return to live with her mother and stay until about three months after the birth. It was inconceivable that a man should have to do his own cooking and cleaning while she was gone and he certainly shouldn't have to sleep alone so he would find a girlfriend. By the time the wife returned the girlfriend would probably be pregnant and so it continued.

The secret to their harmony seemed to be that the two "wives" usually lived on opposite sides of the village or in different villages and didn't meet unnecessarily. Everyone seemed to know who was with whom and who had fathered which children.

We needed our own sturdy truck to transport clients from the boats or the Camp to the departure point for the mekoro. I asked around and was advised that a Samil truck would be best for what we needed. Samils are South African ex-army 4x4 trucks that have strengthened chassis and are ideal for use in wilderness areas.

We found a supplier in South Africa and ordered our truck to be delivered complete with bench seating, a canvas roof cover and sides that could be rolled down on wet days. After a few months of waiting I received word that our truck would be delivered to Gaborone. We had found an experienced driver so four of us set off – me, Rupes, Moleti (the driver) and Double (one of our guides). The trip involved us travelling two hours by motorboat to Sepopa and then eight hours on a bus to Maun. From Maun we took a long six hour bus trip to Francistown and waited to catch the overnight train to Gaborone.

We boarded the train with our snacks and drinks and found seats for the eleven hour trip. I vaguely noted that I was the only white person in the carriage but didn't think much of it as that was how it usually was. A few hours into the trip two very aggressive South African men approached me and demanded to know why I was travelling with the black people. Why wasn't I in a sleeper that white people usually used? I pointed out that we were in Botswana and that everyone is equal in Botswana. After a bit of arguing back and forth and some support from Double (the others had found the bar) they went back to their own seats and left me alone for the rest of the trip. I was a bit shaken by this confrontation. I had been in Botswana two years by then and this was my very first experience of racial prejudice.

On arrival in Gaborone I called the supplier in South Africa and told him we had arrived. The plan had been for us to go straight to the border to meet him and take ownership of the truck there. Unfortunately the driver delivering our truck had turned around and headed back to Pretoria as he realised that he had forgotten to bring the right paperwork to allow us to import the vehicle. He informed me that the handover would be delayed by at least two days and suggested we book into a hotel while we waited. I insisted that this would be at his expense and he agreed.

We pulled over a taxi and drove around trying to find somewhere to stay. I am not sure what conferences, meetings or events were going on in Gaborone that night but we struggled to find anywhere. Eventually we booked into the Gaborone Sun which is quite an expensive hotel. We took two rooms and I made sure that the guys could contact my room if they had any problems. None of them had stayed in such an expensive hotel before and they were a little intimidated. We arranged to meet in the foyer before dinner but before I could make use of the wonderful running water and have a shower, the phone rang and I answered a multitude of questions about things like how to use the air con and how to regulate the mixer taps in the shower. It was easier to just go and show them everything.

The next day we moved to Mokolodi Nature Reserve where they had quite rustic cabins and where we could cook our own meals. I thought it would be great if the polers with me could get to see the white rhinos in this reserve. This was the one big animal that we didn't have in our part of the Delta.

Mokolodi is about 15kms from Gaborone and I knew we would want to drive around the reserve, exploring and looking for rhinos so I hired a car. We went shopping and then out to Mokolodi. Everything went on my credit card as I didn't want anyone at OPT to be able to complain that we used Trust money for our own entertainment.

We ended up staying two nights at Mokolodi as the truck was still not at the border but despite driving around and around and around, we only caught a glimpse of very distant rhinos. We did, however, spend a lot of time watching the Rock Dassies which we also didn't have in the Delta.

The Rock Dassie or Rock Hyrax looks like a large guinea pig with short ears and a short tail. They live in groups of up to eighty, dominated by a large male. They apparently share ancestors with elephants and manatees. We enjoyed watching them basking in the sun on the rocks.

Eventually we received word that the truck would be at the border and we headed off. Once paperwork was completed, we started the long journey back to Seronga. I have glossed over the bureaucracy involved but anyone who has travelled or worked in Africa will understand that the paperwork was extensive and complex and took hours to complete.

I never did get reimbursed for this trip as the person we bought the truck from sent spare parts for the truck in lieu of payment but it was an adventure that we all enjoyed.

Caprivi Strip

We were only just over 100 kilometres from the border with Namibia – into the Caprivi Strip.

The Caprivi Strip is a 400km long narrow strip of land bordered by Botswana, Angola, Zambia and Zimbabwe. Namibia had only gained independence from South Africa after violent conflict in 1990 and in 1999 the CLA (Caprivi Liberation Army – a rebel force) were fighting for succession from Namibia, allegedly supported by UNITA (the Angolan rebel movement).

In August that year the CLA launched attacks on an army base and the Police Station and also occupied the state run radio station in the Caprivi Strip. A state of Emergency was declared and the uprising contained with some violent reprisals. Shortly after, about three thousand people from the Caprivi Strip sought refuge in Botswana.

It was heart wrenching to see the tired, dishevelled families who had walked over two hundred kilometres through bush with just the clothes they stood up in, looking for safety.

Many were San (Bushmen) and they had walked all of the way to Gudigwa – another 70 kilometres from Seronga - looking for sanctuary with relatives and friends. They were rounded up by army trucks, fed, given medical attention and then transferred to the refugee camp at Dukwe in Botswana. They were eventually returned to the Caprivi after the unrest had died down.

There was an incident where four French tourists were killed whilst travelling through the Caprivi Strip as were some aid workers. There were a lot of reports of local people being killed or being taken away, never to be seen again.

Angola was just across the river from the Caprivi Strip and the Namibian Government permitted the Angolan army to mount artillery and rocket attacks from the Caprivi Strip into Angola against the UNITA rebels who had been driven into the South East of Angola. UNITA then retaliated, mounting assaults against vehicles, villages and military bases in the Caprivi Strip. Robberies and assaults were common and UNITA laid landmines in many places. We were told that a regular trick was to hide landmines in piles of elephant dung on the roads.

After a while our SAMIL truck needed to be serviced and there was a mechanic in Rundu in the Caprivi Strip who could do the job. The alternative at that time was to drive it to South Africa. So we contacted the mechanic in Rundu and set off at a time when we knew we wouldn't have too many tourists arriving.

We drove to Mohembo, crossed the Okavango River on the vehicle pontoon and drove the four kilometres to the border post. Unfortunately they wouldn't let us through. Our truck was set up to transport tourists but as an ex- army vehicle painted green, it could easily be mistaken for an army vehicle and it was just too dangerous for us to travel along the Caprivi Strip. We had to turn around and head back to Seronga.

We waited a couple of months until things had calmed down a little and then painted our logo with the hippo picture all over the vehicle and tried again. This time we were allowed to proceed. We had to spend four days in Rundu while the truck was serviced and then went home.

Whenever we made a trip outside Seronga, we were inundated with requests for lifts from all members of the community and were happy to oblige whenever we could. On this occasion most got off the truck at Mohembo to carry on to Shakawe, Maun or other villages along the way. On this particular trip we also took two of the guides and a boat driver with us as they just wanted to visit Namibia. It was whilst helping them fill out forms at the border that I understood:

The country is Botswana. One person is a Motswana. A group of people are Batswana. The national language is Setswana.

Later we found a truck mechanic in Maun who could work on the SAMIL but sourcing parts was always a challenge.

At one time Moleti was worried that the truck needed some work so we set off for Maun. We got across the river and then we started having real problems with the drive shaft. We had to stop twice while Moleti and the others travelling with us made some temporary repairs and then we drove on very slowly. By this time it was starting to get dark and it was obvious we weren't going to make it to Maun that day.

We eventually made it to Gumare where Moleti assured us he had family who would look after us for the night. His family were wonderful. They welcomed us with open arms, finding all eight of us food and then insisting that I sleep in their house in their real bed. I was embarrassed and tried to insist that I could happily stay with the others but was advised that they would be offended if I didn't take them up on their offer. A child brought me a basin of warm water to wash with and a towel and I gratefully settled down to sleep.

The next day in daylight Moleti was able to make some more repairs and we headed off. His family refused all offers to pay for the food we had eaten. This was typical Batswana hospitality. All visitors are welcomed and treated like honoured guests.

Traditional Meals and Non-traditional Movies

We offered visiting groups the opportunity to enjoy a traditional meal and dancing in the campsite on their return from camping on an island in the Delta. The meal consisted of: fresh fish cooked with water lilies; bread cooked on the campfire; maize meal or samp; and vegetables such as pumpkin, cabbage or chowmolia (a local form of kale). Khadi was also available to sample.

All ingredients were sourced locally and cooked by women from the village. This again helped to provide some income for the women.

For the dancing we borrowed or hired large drums and we had two polers who could play the kowaware – a traditional musical instrument made from a bow and string with the sound regulated by movement of air in the cheek and from the mouth. Most traditional songs in Botswana are accompanied only by the clapping of hands and the banging of sticks but the drums provided more impressive and haunting accompaniment.

Five or six women from the village donned the bulky skirts made of reeds which rattled and swirled as they danced. They were good at getting the visitors to join in and it was a great experience around a roaring fire.

I had hoped that the Camp bar/restaurant could operate as a community resource. It was especially well patronised by the police and teachers who appreciated the chance to eat out and to socialise in a bar more like what they were used to in their home towns and who also had disposable income. I think that visitors enjoyed mixing with locals.

We bought a TV and video player to set up in the bar and used the generator to run film nights. I was excited to buy a copy of the Lion King when I was in Australia. I really thought that the polers and others from the village would enjoy seeing the animals with their realistic behaviours and movements. I had not anticipated that they would be insulted.

"Why are you trying to make us watch a children's movie?" they asked angrily. I explained that the Lion King was popular with all ages and was backed up by a young backpacker who said "I love the Lion King. It is my favourite movie. I would like to watch it".

So I put it on. The locals watched only half-heartedly and after a few minutes I asked them if they wanted me to turn it off. They quickly agreed.

The usual movie that was popular had plenty of action and usually featured Jackie Chan or some other martial arts heroes. I had unfortunately seen too many of these on long bus trips between Maun and Gaborone where the sound was usually absent or unintelligible. I genuinely thought that the polers would enjoy The Lion King but they were clearly offended and thought I was insulting them. Who knew? Once again cultural differences took me by surprise.

Health and Healing

Traditional healers still pay an important part in the lives of the villagers. They are consulted on all ailments and for advice on disputes and family problems.

There is a medical clinic in Seronga but while I was there it was not well equipped. Nurses are sent to work there – often thousands of kilometres from their homes – and their resentment was sometimes obvious. My experience was that they usually dispensed paracetamol, vitamin C and malaria medication only. I think that the nurses were well trained and they would tell people what they should use or take but then they had to add "but we don't have any". I imagine that it wasn't very satisfying work for them.

We ended up with quite a comprehensive First Aid Kit at the camp and I had some amusing moments when polers would come for help with a variety of ailments.

O.C. came into the office one day and told me that one of the polers needed my help. I asked him what was wrong but he just ushered the poler in and closed the door as he left the room.

The poler, who didn't speak much English, dropped his pants and presented his sore penis to me. I managed to act as if this wasn't in the least unusual, put on latex gloves, administered antiseptic cream and suggested he go to the clinic. O.C thought it was hilarious.

On another occasion Sikiri, the caretaker, arrived with a bite on his thigh. He had been cheating on his wife and they had fought. She bit him. Another time she hit him with a spade and cut him quite badly. He wasn't at all bitter about these wounds as he felt he deserved them. Sikiri was always cheerful and good to work with and had a real impish air about him.

Most treatments I administered involved antiseptics and bandages. I used to buy multi-vitamins from Maun in huge jars and dish these out to all the polers. I also regularly brought numerous boxes of condoms back from the Council office in Maun and made them readily available in the bar and reception areas.

Botswana has one of the highest rates of HIV infection in the world. When I arrived I found that people were in total denial. Lots of younger adults were dying and when I asked what had been wrong with them the explanations were usually along the lines of "She had a headache." Or "He had a stomach ache". It was considered a great insult to suggest that someone might have had AIDS.

The Government of Botswana was doing its best to educate people but it seemed that people absorbed the knowledge but thought it had nothing to do with them. I heard about workshops that had been run for men at various kgotlas. I was told that at one some of the older men were so disgusted when the presenter tried to demonstrate how to put on a condom that they literally picked up their chairs, turned around and sat with their backs to him.

Educators were also fighting against the ingrained belief that a man should be able to have sex with whomever he wished and that having children was an essential requirement of a successful relationship. Having said that however, I noticed that many Bayei families were limited to 2 or 3 children with female contraception being acceptable.

Free condoms were readily available at the Clinic and in towns they were even on the counter at banks but it was going to take some time for young males to accept that condoms weren't some insult to their virility.

I thought it was sad that it seemed that a whole generation was dying. This was the 25 - 40 years old who were still very sexually active but who had also had some education. Their children ended up being raised by less educated grandparents who often had health issues of their own with TB being rife. I worried that this was bound to put back the advancement of Botswana.

By the time I returned to Australia I had already seen a change in attitude towards HIV infection and the Government was screening all pregnant women to avoid mother to child infection. Anti-retroviral drugs were available for free.

Witchcraft and superstition still affect the lives of the people in the Delta.

Not long after I arrived I was sitting in Willie's campsite talking to one of the more westernised young guides, Gully. He was explaining to me how lots of people still believed in witchcraft but assured me that he didn't. A short time later I asked him about how he received the large scar that stood out right across one cheek. He explained that he received it from an attack by a buffalo and that this buffalo had been sent by an enemy to attack him through witchcraft.

Sometimes polers would come and explain that they had to return to their village because they weren't feeling well. They believed that they were unwell because they hadn't visited their parents. I told my own children about this belief and suggested they might like to adopt it!

Sareqo was also one of the older polers. Again he was short but quite stocky with a cheerful round face and beard. I once heard a tour group referring to him as Poppa Smurf and realised that Poppa Smurf was exactly who he looked like.

Although he was an experienced guide Sareqo was finding the physical effort needed to guide a safari quite challenging. He approached a number of other members and told them that as he was Chairman of the Board he should get a job in the camp. With no skills to do office work or housekeeping or cooking, there really wasn't a job for him. The long-term plan was to establish an information centre/museum at the camp and he would be the ideal person to run this. But the centre didn't yet exist.

Some of the staff and other Board Members came to tell me that they believed that Sareqo was a wizard and that he might hurt them or their families if he didn't get a job. I told them that I wasn't afraid of witchcraft and that they should just blame me. The instant retort of "Oh no! You are too important to us!" was flattering but I was still faced with the dilemma of what to do with Sareqo.

Whenever I got the chance I discussed it with workers from some of the community development agencies that worked in the Delta but even the most educated were worried that there might be consequences.

In the end I stood my ground but certainly didn't increase my popularity with Sareqo. It was hard to maintain my integrity of doing what is best for all in the face of traditional beliefs and self-interest.

Xao / Seronga

There was ongoing pressure from the Xao polers and ongoing resistance from the Seronga polers. Because we had the Camp at Seronga it was important to use it as a base. We wanted to encourage visitors to use the bar and restaurant and to buy baskets so, whenever possible, we needed to leave from Mbiroba. Departures and arrivals from Xao also required much more use of vehicles and the continuing challenge of maintaining fuel supplies.

One year while I was away the polers continued finishing trips at Xao long after they should have started using Mbiroba again. The mekoro had been cut off by rising flood levels and we had to hire Willie's tractor and trailer to transport all the mekoro back.

Family Visits

Every year I flew home at the end of November and spent Christmas with my family but this year I was going home early to attend my daughter's wedding. I spent the night at Island Safari Lodge and as I pulled on my t-shirt the next morning, I felt a sharp "prick" on my stomach. I had a quick look, hoping it wasn't a spider but I couldn't see a wound or a culprit so I assumed it was a mosquito bite.

Travelling home in those days involved a long trip – a hot, bumpy eight-hour drive from Seronga to Maun (or a two-hour motor boat trip and then 8 hours on a bus or hitch-hiking); staying overnight in Maun and then travelling by bus the 1000kms to Gaborone. Then it was on another bus to Johannesburg to overnight at a backpackers and then to the airport to wait for the seventeen hour flight home.

This trip was to improve considerably when finances allowed me to fly from Maun to Johannesburg and when the lovely people at Mack Air would give me a lift on a plane from Seronga to Maun (only 45 minutes).

In the future Qantas would also adjust their flight path and reduce the flying time to a mere 12 ½ hours but at the time my daughter was getting married it took me almost four days to get home and by the time I got off the plane in Sydney my "mosquito bite" was really painful. It wasn't constantly sore but every few minutes I experienced a really sharp pain – bad enough to stop me in my tracks as I was walking. The area was red and swollen and painful to touch.

I thought I should get it checked out and went to the Medical Centre. I don't know if it was my scruffy appearance or the wound but the Doctor sat on his side of the desk and didn't examine the wound as I pulled up my shirt and explained that I thought I had an infected mosquito bite. He prescribed antibiotic cream and told me to keep it covered.

Two days later I was changing the dressing when a very large maggot popped out on the bandaid. It was the larva of a putse fly.

Putse fly are well-known in Africa for laying their eggs on domestic animals. Experienced people always iron everything that comes off the washing line in case it has putse fly eggs on it. I knew that but thought I had read somewhere that there are no putse flies in the Okavango Delta. That obviously isn't true. The pain I had felt was the putse maggot eating my flesh. It had hollowed out an abscess and was chomping away. I still have the scar today.

By sheer luck, the antibiotic cream and the band aid on the wound was the right treatment. Putse maggots need to breathe air and the common remedy is to apply Vaseline and when the maggot moves to the surface to try to breathe, squeeze it out.

Of course I excitedly told my family but asked them not to mention it to other people as it seemed a bit repulsive. They assured me that they wouldn't tell people but as I heard one of their friends refer to me as "maggot woman" and another to accuse me of illegally importing animals into Australia, they obviously couldn't resist telling.

My daughter Eleanor, her husband and my four year old grandson Matthew, came to visit me when I still lived in Seronga Village and was helping the Trust to build Mbiroba Camp.

My living conditions were good by village standards but some-what primitive by Australian standards. I lived in one room made of concrete blocks and with a corrugated iron roof. It was quite luxurious in that it had a large window. It was owned by Rupes' cousin - who had attended Harvard University to do post-graduate studies and was practicing law in Gaborone.

I was continually coming across people who had come from remote disadvantaged communities but had managed to achieve so much. In Botswana, people seem to have supreme confidence that they can be and do whatever they want. It can be a bit of a disadvantage sometimes when a gardener or cleaner applies for an accountant or Manager's job, fully believing that if they are not qualified, they can be trained. Mind you, many of the workers at the camp did prove that they could achieve a lot if given the opportunity.

Moeletsi's house had two separate rooms. I lived in one and he and his family would come and stay in the other room from time to time. I paid no rent but did maintenance on the house as it was needed and built a reed fence to provide a private enclosure around the front of the building. I also tried to arrange to have a tap installed in the yard but nothing happens quickly in Botswana and this didn't happen until after I had moved out.

The river was quite close and when the floods were in, I would fetch water from the river to use. Otherwise, I had to use a vehicle and fill a large blue plastic drum for my water supply.

Families were delighted if they could get hold of large plastic cooking oil containers which they would clean thoroughly using sand and water and then use to collect and store water. In the evenings there would be a long queue of young children or women lining up at the stand pipes with their containers to fetch water and I would join them.

I must say that during my three and a half years living in the village, it never worried me that I didn't have electricity but I often used to think how great it would be to have a tap with running water. Sometimes I would arrive home after a long and busy day and remember that I didn't have much water. It certainly isn't recommended to go near the river at night because of the crocodiles and hippos and so it would be a toss-up as to whether I would wash or use the water to cook with.

Many a time the prospect of lighting a fire to cook with and having no water to wash in saw me eating cold baked beans out of the tin, or just having a dry piece of bread. Life became a little easier when I bought a small gas bottle and screw on cook top so at least I didn't have to fetch firewood to cook.

When my family arrived in Seronga they flew in as we thought the long, hot journey by road would be hard with a four year old (at least with a Western four year old). I did many eight hour road trips with very small local children who never ever whinged and cried. They also didn't need constant entertainment or distraction but our children seem to be used to constant attention.

I had warned the family to be prepared to rough it and they took things really well. It was like a camping adventure for them to fetch water, find firewood etc. We washed in a tin bath, used a long-drop toilet and used a paraffin lamp or candles for lighting. One night El, Matt and I walked into the one-room house together and as we did so, I heard the rustle of a plastic bag. I looked in the direction of the sound just in time to see the tail end of a snake slither past. Once again I went to fetch Simon who brought his stick and his gun this time. It took ages to find the snake as it was curled up on top of a cupboard. By the time we found it, we had removed all the furniture, clothes etc. out of the room onto the sand outside. Once again, a dangerous cobra had come to visit.

I took the family by motorboat to visit Guma Lagoon Fishing Camp, run by Nookie and Geoff Randall. The Trust bought all their fibreglass mekoro from Geoff, and Geoff and Nookie had been wonderfully supportive to me through a lot of my learning experiences.

They invited us to lunch and I thought it would be great for my family to experience a bit of luxury and to have the wonderful experience of travelling by boat along the channels of the Okavango River. We set off early as it usually took about one and a half hours to get there and we were expected for lunch but unfortunately the channel through the papyrus hadn't been used recently and was incredibly overgrown so it took us about three hours of crashing through the overgrown waterway before we arrived.

Lunch was fantastic with lots of fresh vegetables that we never saw in Seronga and interrupted only by the shooting of a deadly Black Mamba that hung above us in the trees while we ate.

The third snake that visited me at home came when the floods were arriving and the snakes were being disturbed from the river banks.

Once again, I walked into my room just in time to see the end of a tail disappear under the bed. I wasn't actually sure if it was a snake or a lizard as I saw only the tip of its tail but I wasn't taking any chances. I had no vehicle and Simon wasn't in the village anyway so I went to the nearby Seventh Day Adventist Church where many of my neighbours had gathered and asked for help. Four or five men came and hunted down and killed the snake for me. I wasn't sure how that fitted in with their interrupted church service but I was grateful.

The other snake adventure we had was in Mbiroba Camp. We were often getting snakes in the guest chalets. They had nice warm thatched rooves and were near the river. But this one came into the restaurant kitchen.

It was a Black Mamba. A bite from this snake can kill a grown man in one hour so we were all pretty nervous. Eventually one of the staff threw a spear at it. It went through the snake, attaching it to the roof. Unfortunately, its body was pinned to the roof in the bar but its front half and head was still very much alive in the kitchen next door.

We had guests arriving for dinner but the chef, understandably, was refusing to start cooking with the snake up above him. It was quite a performance to kill this snake twenty feet above our heads. Normally, I tried to encourage the staff and polers not to kill all these animals they were wary of, but in this case it had to be done.

It was wonderful for me to have my family see where I lived and to meet the people I worked with every day.

We went on mekoro far into the Delta with one of the guides called Double and another poler. El was really nervous as she sat in the mokoro with young Matt. If it wasn't dodging all the low hanging spider webs, or surprise visits from little Reed Frogs, it was the grunting of the hippos who sounded so close.

We had a restful stay on one of the remote islands and a guided walk. The next night we stayed on another small island closer to Seronga and pitched the tents under some trees. The guides built a fire and dug a latrine pit.

We were all asleep early and I was woken in the dark of night by a ting ting noise. Peeping out of the tent flap I saw Double and the other guide up by the fire, feeding more wood onto it and tapping gently on a pot lid. I realised that our tents were surrounded by large elephants, gently pulling leaves from the branches above us. I noticed that the guides were just in their underwear and, with perfect faith in their ability to look after us, lay down and went back to sleep.

I woke a while later to see the fire had been really banked up, the ting ting had become a bang bang on the pot lids and the Guides were fully dressed. The elephants weren't too worried about us. They stepped gently over all the tent guy ropes and made no noise as they walked around. When we got up the next morning we could see that they had been everywhere over the campsite. My family slept through it all.

We also did a trip to Chobe where we did some game drives and a river cruise where we were able to get really close to the elephants and hippos. I scoffed at El's nervousness about going near the river in the campsite where large signs warned us about the crocodiles but only weeks after they left a tourist camping near the water was dragged into the water by a large crocodile while still in her tent.

Earlier in the week we had visited the Crocodile Farm near Maun and commented on the broken fences and the crocodile slide marks outside the fenced area. I assured the family that it was safer than it looked but literally the next week a man who worked at the Farm was taken by a crocodile that had come through a hole in the fence. Coincidentally the man was from Seronga Village. Maybe I was the one getting too used to the wildlife!

I took Matt with me to the rubbish tip that had recently been established outside Seronga. It was just a hole in the ground with a wire mesh fence around it. The rubbish was proper rubbish – not like when I was a child when going to the tip was an opportunity to search for discarded treasures. But we did come across a large elephant tooth which Matt carried around for the rest of his stay. I made him throw it away just before he left as I was worried that it would be detected at the airport and he might be in trouble for having ivory.

Matt also had fun exploring and found a large frog which was hibernating in the sand, waiting for the rains to return.

A dog had its puppies under a bush in my yard and Matt really enjoyed playing with them. For years after he would ask how the puppies were and it was a long time before I admitted that they had all died from putse fly infestation a few weeks after he left.

Towards the end of their stay, we all then headed off to Zimbabwe where we did all the usual touristy things - got drenched at Vic Falls, bought carvings, ate great food and where (according to

Matt's recollections) a crocodile ate Matt's sunglasses. I think that the truth was that El had the sunglasses hooked into her shirt and Matt in her arms so he could see the huge croc rear up to grab the meat dangled from a pole above it. As she bent over slightly, the sunglasses fell into the croc's pool. Matt couldn't believe that she wouldn't go down to retrieve them.

It was a wonderful visit and I love that we have some shared memories of Botswana.

Animal Adventures

Mice were always a bit of a nuisance. I was quite willing to share a little food with the mice I shared my room with although they were always waking me with loud chewing noises, even chewing my clothes. One night one even woke me up when she pulled hairs from my head. I think she thought my blonde hair was nice coarse straw or dried grass to build her nest with. I woke up and shone my torch on her sitting calmly on my pillow and she just sat there looking at me.

Some of the mice were actually really cute with big ears and big eyes and they weren't really scared of people either. I couldn't kill any of them and I used to chase them out of the open door. They probably just came back of course. Rupes was no tougher than me and would help me "herd" them out the door.

When we had a plague of mice in the food store room at the camp, one of the female kitchen staff had no trouble cornering each one and dispatching them by hitting them on the head with the handle of a large knife. I helped round them up, and didn't mind disposing of the bodies but just couldn't kill them.

One year we had an absolute plague of caterpillars in the house. They came from the trees outside and would swarm everywhere in the room, over clothes, and over the bed when we were away at work. They left fine, spiky hairs behind which caused immediate welts and rashes when they came in touch with skin. You couldn't see where the caterpillars had been so it was almost impossible to avoid contact with the hairs.

After returning from work and coming into the room Rupes and I were both in agony and rushed to change our clothes and wash our skin. Unfortunately the caterpillars had also crawled across the towels and we just increased our exposure. This invasion only lasted a few days but it was awful.

Being caught up in a tourism business and dealing with normal business matters all the time, it was sometimes easy to forget that I was in Africa. But then I would be reminded. Polers would disappear to hunt lions that had killed their cattle, villagers walking home would be killed by elephants, and sadly, babies would die from things that never killed children in the western world any more.

Every year people from Seronga or nearby villages were killed by elephants and children were taken by crocodiles. I met people who had been attacked by lions, by leopards or by buffaloes – and they had the scars to prove it.

On one occasion three large male lions wandered through Seronga during the night when we were all asleep. Their tracks went right down the main street and they obviously went to the river for a drink.

Small herds of elephants would come splashing into the river near the Camp in the late afternoon, looking to drink their fill of water. We often heard the "thunderflashes" that the Wildlife Department would fire off to discourage the elephants from coming right into the village.

A bachelor group of three buffaloes walked down the fence line of the Camp very early each morning on their way to the river.

Some clients became very complacent about the hazards of wild animals. Often they had been to Kruger National Park in South Africa or Etosha in Namibia before arriving in the Delta and had seen a lot of animals that were used to seeing people in these busy parks. They came to regard the animals as exhibits almost and didn't understand that in Seronga we lived with the wildlife on their terms.

Funerals and Weddings

Funerals were frequent but I only attended if it was for someone I knew well. Sometimes I would stay behind at the Camp to meet groups, organise pick-ups etc. to allow other staff members to attend a burial.

On one occasion early in my time in Botswana one of our polers died and I went to his family compound to pay my respects. I was greeted by a senior male member of the family and introduced to a young woman who spoke good English and would translate for me, where necessary. She explained to me that I needed to cover my arms and wear a scarf. I had dressed in a skirt and modest blouse but hadn't realised that this wasn't enough.

The girl ran off and returned with a thick woollen jacket which she helped me put on. She then led me to the area where all the older women were sitting on the ground outside a hut and explained that she had to go and help with the food. She spoke to another woman who brought me a large scarf and my neighbour on the ground showed me how to wind it around and around my head and tie it securely. It was 40oC plus and there I was sitting on the hot sand in a woollen jacket and thick headscarf!

After a while I saw that the women were getting up in small groups and walking into the hut. I realised that they were going to view the body. I tried to politely decline the invitation to join them but was gently encouraged onto my feet and followed the women into the darkened hut.

This was only the second funeral I had ever been to and I was quite confronted by the thought of seeing a dead person. Lying on the bed, with a sheet pulled up to his chin he looked peaceful, as if he was just asleep.

I never saw my "translator" again but was well looked after by the other women who made sure I received food and drink with them.

This was not to be my last experience with bodies. At the time the closest mortuary was in Gumare – 100kms on a sand road, over the river on the pontoon and then another 140kms on the tar road to Gumare. There weren't many vehicles in the village and often people didn't have much petrol so we would be approached to help transport a body to Gumare. If we could, we helped.

I remember one particular time when the body was placed in the back of the land cruiser surrounded by close family members and we set off. When we got to Gumare they informed us that the mortuary was full. A quick phone call was made to the Community Trust who had one of the few phones in Seronga, asking them to contact the family back in Seronga to tell them to start digging the grave.

In the heat, time was of the essence and we now had to make the return trip. We also had to make sure we got to the pontoon before it stopped operating at 6pm. On many occasions we had arrived late and had to sleep at the pontoon and got absolutely ravished by mosquitoes.

Otherwise we would return to Shakawe to find accommodation. It would then be a rush first thing in the morning to get back to the river to get the first pontoon and avoid the sometimes long queue of vehicles. I am eternally grateful to Eileen Drotsky from Drotskys cabins who always made me welcome if I was stranded. On this occasion, however, we made it on time.

It was not uncommon to see bakkies with bodies on the back. The headlights would be turned on and people would bow their heads respectfully as the vehicle passed.

Another sad trip was to pick up the body of a baby from the mortuary at Gumare. On arrival the parents knocked on the mortuary door, went inside for less than five minutes and returned with a little wrapped bundle. They sat on the back of the land cruiser holding their baby all the way back to Seronga.

The Okavango Community Trust (OCT) had entered into an agreement with a safari company as part of the Government CBNRM (Community Based Natural Resource Management Program) that was designed to allow communities to receive benefit from neighbouring wildlife areas where they were no longer allowed to hunt or to have their cattle.

As part of their incentive to get OCT to partner with them, MacFarlane Safaris had promised to provide the community with a mortuary. This they finally did by providing a large freezer. Unfortunately they didn't supply the generator or staff to allow the mortuary to operate and I often cursed them as we saw families struggle to get a body to Gumare so they could arrange the funeral. The transport usually cost them money as well.

Relatives were often far away and time had to be allowed for them to get to Seronga by public transport so funerals had to be delayed.

On numerous occasions I joined the community in paying my respects by visiting the home of the grieving family. From what I understood, six months after the death, the close family would gather again to have a hand washing ceremony, often involving the cutting of hair and culminating in the distribution of the deceased's personal possessions.

One burial I went to I saw the widow helped to the graveside by female relatives. She was covered with a sheet and was loudly crying. This is a society where people are allowed to grieve fully. None of our stupid stiff upper lip. They can be completely distraught and supported by family until they then need to get on with their everyday lives.

I found it especially sad to hear when a baby had died – often from malaria.

On a trip back from Xao we were pulled over by a man who explained that his wife was having twins and she was in difficulties. We drove to their small settlement and picked up the woman, laying her on camping mattresses we had in the back. She was not near full term in her pregnancy and was bleeding quite a lot. I drove her to the Clinic but was told that the midwife was at another village over the river and they couldn't help her. Despite my protests I had to take her to relatives in Seronga. I had been told that the midwife was due back that evening so every hour or so I would drive back to the Clinic to see if she had returned. By nine o'clock it was clear that she wouldn't be back as the pontoon closed at six and motorboats were very reluctant to travel on the river at night.

She arrived back the next day and immediately called for an aeroplane to evacuate the poor woman. I heard that she gave birth on the plane and lost both babies.

We wanted the members (and owners) of the Trust to have as much benefit as they could from their involvement. Obviously they had the opportunity to work but we also arranged for each member to be covered by Funeral Insurance. Funerals were a real financial challenge for families and deaths from illness were becoming more and more common. After filling in a lot of paperwork, each month the Trust would pay the monthly premium for all the members. The hope was that they would carry on with these payments after our subsidies from CEDA finished.

Weddings in Botswana are very expensive and can take years to plan. The bride and groom's aunts and uncles make all the preparations, starting with protracted discussions between the families as to where, when and how.

The weddings I saw were usually a mixture of western and customary traditions. The bride wore a white wedding dress and there were up to ten bridesmaids and ten groomsmen – depending on the wealth of the family. Celebrations went on for about five days with all of the wedding party in different outfits for each day. The ceremony itself is usually a civil matter, presided over by the District Commissioner or a religious ceremony at one of the many churches.

Food must be provided each day. The invited guests include family, friends and village dignitaries but anyone can come to a wedding and expect to be fed.

The groom is very formally dressed and must always remain serious. He wears white gloves and a formal hat and is closely attended by his best man at all times.

The bride is brought to the groom by her family who sing, dance and ululate (the loud wailing with tongue movements used to express joy or grief) from her family home to the wedding venue. These days she is usually transported in the back of a bakkie (ute/ pickup truck). She and guests will often drive around the village loudly singing and laughing in delight after the ceremony.

I attended the wedding of Rupes' sister in Maun and my gift to them was wedding photos. In the morning I took many photos of the family and the ceremony and was able to get them developed and in an album before the evening celebrations began. This was a huge novelty and was really well received.

The family was wonderful and included me in all aspects of the wedding with the Bride's family including helping the bride to get dressed. I had been to weddings in the village where I was treated as an honoured guest but this was the first time I really felt part of it.

AGM

The conflict between the Xao and Seronga factions came to a head at an AGM when we were still building the camp. Kepaletswe was elected Chairman and, as his first show of power, demanded that I stand before him at the AGM while he laid down the law. It was a hot, dry day and as the camp was only partially built we had laid out rows of white plastic chairs under the thatched roof of the polers building. The new Board – heavily weighted by Xao polers - sat facing the polers behind large white plastic tables.

Kepaletswe directed all his comments to me. He spoke aggressively and while I waited for translation (although I had caught the gist of what he was saying) I knew from his tone that he wasn't happy. He pointed out that he was the boss and that I must do what he told me. I felt quite confronted and hoped that the meeting would soon finish.

I knew that his problem was that I was blamed for blocking the move of the base to Xao but his attack felt so personal. I frequently had to defend my position to use some of the money paid by tourists for safaris to keep the camp operating and to plan for the future. I found that there was no commitment to planning or saving for the future and I understood that life is precarious in this part of the world and the future can't be counted on but it was a hard way to establish and run a business.

I think that night I began to question whether I would stay.

Baskets

It was important to us all that as many people as possible gained from the Trust and our safari business. Our polers were all men and so one way of 'spreading the wealth' was to provide an outlet for the women who made baskets.

The art of basket making in Botswana was enhanced by the arrival of Hambukushu refugees from Angola in 1967. These refugees were escaping from the violent civil war and were welcomed by the people of Botswana and its Government who settled them in the thirteen Etsha Villages on the other side of the River. (I loved that the villages were unimaginatively named Etsha 1, Etsha 2 etc up to Etsha 13) The Hambukushu brought their basket making skills with them and added the Bayei knowledge of traditional materials and dyes to make beautiful and useful baskets. The women in our village were never idle. If they were sitting, they were usually making baskets.

Anne had been buying some baskets and re-selling them in Maun but she couldn't buy all that were produced and, as a businesswoman, had to get something back by requiring that the women purchase something from her shop if she bought a basket from them.

To avoid having women turn up daily, every few weeks I would let the office staff know what day I would be buying baskets but that I wouldn't be starting until 8am. Word spread quickly and women and girls would come from all the villages along our side of the river, and by the time I got up at 6am a long queue had already formed along the road.

I tried to buy as many baskets as I could, often buying some baskets that weren't really up to standard to encourage the young girls to keep improving their skills. Each time I would buy at least a hundred baskets which we would then display for sale to visiting tourists.

From time to time I would take half a dozen black garbage bags jammed full of baskets to sell in Maun to safari companies or local shops.

The Trust

The Okavango Polers Trust was registered in June 1998. Its aim was *"To offer an affordable trip to allow more people to enjoy the Delta and to provide more jobs in this disadvantaged, economically impoverished rural area."*

Anne Clift-Hill was an Englishwoman living with Willie Phillips who was a well-known Professional Hunter in Botswana. The first time I met Willie he immediately told me "I am a coloured man". Having been raised in multi-cultural Wellington in New Zealand this really didn't mean anything to me but over time I understood that Willie's background growing up as a coloured in South Africa had shaped many of his ideas and attitudes.

By the time he moved to Seronga in the 1990s Willie was much more of a conservationist than a hunter and he and Anne initiated a number of projects that helped the local communities. They were running a mobile shop on their 10 tonne Scania truck, visiting all the villages and settlements south of Seronga. They also operated a shop from two shipping containers in the middle of Seronga.

They had helped to organise and install water bores at Eretsha and had helped start the Okavango Polers Trust (OPT).

The OPT was started in response to an enquiry from Paul Sheller and Ann Uren from Audi Camp who wanted to provide low cost mokoro safaris for budget travellers. Mekoro were the usual form of transport along the waterways and between islands in the area and there were a lot of experienced polers who welcomed the opportunity to work for themselves. Anne helped to register the Trust and the small group I arrived with were the first paying group to go on safari with the Trust.

Anne was known as MaWillie. If she had children she would have been named Ma and whatever the name of her firstborn was. For instance if I had my family in Botswana my name would have changed from Sue to MaEleanor.

Anne was the Treasurer of OPT until we received some Government funding that required all members to be citizens and she wasn't a citizen at that time. Anne's experience and commercial approach guided the Trust ably.

With her gruff demeanour and constant swearing many people thought that Willie was the friendly one with all the philanthropic ideas but I learnt that this simply wasn't true. Willie had many good ideas and supported all their projects but it was always up to Anne to make things happen. I discovered a woman with a heart of gold and the energy and devotion to thrive in the challenging environment of such a remote location. I admire her greatly.

I was happy to celebrate Anne and Willie's wedding with the whole community and many visitors from Maun. Unfortunately not long after this a violent drunken attack on Anne by Willie made me wary of being involved so much with them socially.

Anne and Willie helped buy the first five fibreglass mekoro and we carried on that practice by buying and registering fibreglass mekoro which the polers paid off with their earnings over the following year to eighteen months.

Many of the Trust members had worked for safari companies and they were keen to present the professional image that those companies did. As funds became available we purchased uniforms for all the camp staff and polers with our Polers Trust logo proudly attached. I was then asked to take photos of all the staff in their new uniforms, posing with beautiful baskets.

Once Mbiroba Camp was built we provided the following employment:

75 poler members; 4 women catering traditional dinners; 8-15 traditional dancers and singers; 2 drivers; 2 office workers; an Assistant Manager; a Business Manager; 3 caretakers/guards; up to 30 casual polers and labourers; 4 housekeeping staff; and 2 laundry ladies.

In addition work was provided for motorboat operators, women collecting reeds, basket makers and many others. The shops and bar in the village benefitted with increased sales and, whenever possible, our vehicles were used to give people lifts and to provide transport.

I first arrived as a volunteer but after six months I had to approach the Board and ask for some payment as I was running out of money. Then after nearly four years working for the Trust I asked for a salary equivalent to what Camp Managers were receiving from the larger safari companies. Part of the reason behind this request was to help prepare the Trust for what they would have to pay if they recruited a new Manager. We were really living in a bit of a bubble with the subsidies from the Government and the situation wasn't sustainable.

Our biggest challenge with using our vehicles was that they were needed constantly, especially in the dry season, and we had to really manage our fuel supplies. We were so grateful to Malcolm Thomas at the Etsha Co-op and the OCT who helped with fuel on many occasions.

There weren't many vehicles in the village and we gave lifts to Shakawe and to Maun whenever we could. I remember one time when we picked up a whole bakkie load of little old people. Apparently they were going to Shakawe to get their pensions.

At every little settlement we would stop and pick up one or two very frail old people waiting on the side of the road who would need to be helped onto the back and settled as safely and comfortably as possible. I was driving that day and so nervous that if I hit a bump too hard, they might all end up with broken bones.

Botswana Day

The main buildings at Mbiroba Camp were nearly completed and we wanted to celebrate with all the polers, and indeed the whole village, so it was decided that we would cater for Botswana Day celebrations at the Camp Restaurant.

We bought a cow and a few goats which were slaughtered out the back of the restaurant kitchen. A group of tourists passing through at the time heard what was happening and asked to be allowed to watch. With a mixture of fascination and horror they watched the animals bled, skinned and butchered. Nothing was wasted. I noticed that most of the group found the process confronting and didn't hang around long.

Four large three-legged pots were borrowed from the Primary School and cooking went on all day.

More than two hundred people arrived to enjoy the celebration. As was usual, the older men were fed first, ate quickly and asked for second helpings before we had served everyone else. I said that they had to wait. They weren't too happy about this but I was concerned that we would run out of food as more and more men kept arriving.

I was apparently asked if the older men could have the offal that was in one pot and which is considered a delicacy. I obviously wasn't clear in my communication as my decision to make the older men wait was interpreted as "No-one is to eat the offal". I didn't realise and moved on to the next thing requiring my attention. We were totally rushed off our feet trying to wash plates as they were emptied as we didn't have enough for such a large crowd. We also gave each diner a non-alcoholic drink so the bar was frantically busy as well.

The next day I was called in front of the Board to explain why I had wasted food. It didn't escape my attention that the most disgruntled Board members were those most loudly demanding second helpings the previous day. Unfortunately the pot of cooked offal had been left out all night and had begun to ferment. It was indeed wasted!

After some discussion the Board announced that I was to be fined five goats because of the wastage. I argued that this was a misunderstanding not any malice on my part and eventually the fine was cancelled.

Blackie

One Sunday afternoon I arrived home to find a very cute little black puppy that Rupes said had arrived from another village on a mokoro. Because it was Sunday and because it was black, Rupes named him Black Sabbath but he would always be known as Blackie.

I was really in two minds about having a dog. I loved the idea of having a dog but was always aware that at some time I would have to leave Botswana. I have always considered dogs forever pets and it felt a bit irresponsible to take on a pet when I might not be there forever.

But Blackie was irresistible and became an important part of my life. Village dogs are just so easy. We never had to toilet train him and he was really well behaved. One day I raised my voice at him when he came into the house all wet and sandy and sat on the rug. He sloped off outside and never sat on the mat again. He didn't like to sleep inside at night and would lie outside my bedroom window. He was a great watchdog as well.

When I moved into the Manager's House at Mbiroba Camp he wandered around and was no trouble except with one poler when he was a small puppy. He had grabbed the man's flapping pant leg as he passed by and had ripped a small hole with his sharp little teeth. The poler lashed out, kicking and hitting Blackie. I was so angry. I was happy to replace the damaged trousers but was shocked at the violent outburst.

One of the saddest things I had to do when I left Botswana was to part with Blackie. We had been together over five years by that stage and he was such a good dog. Pierre and Desiree offered to take him and I knew they would treat him well. After a while they gave him to a lady known as "Gogs" who had a few dogs and was happy to have one more.

Hunting

There was talk that our area would be opened up to hunting. This would ruin the Trust's photographic safaris so we tried to mobilise all the villages and settlements in our area to present a united front to the Government. This involved us holding a Kgotla meeting at all the villages from Seronga to Gudigwa. I found it fascinating to participate in these meetings.

Kgotla meetings are always long as everyone who wants to speak must be allowed to. The men sit at the front, often on traditional wooden and string hand-crafted Kgotla chairs that they bring with them but as time went on we saw more and more plastic chairs being used.

The women sit on the ground at the back or to the side of the men's group, with the children. They are able to participate in the discussion if they want to.

When we drove up to one village a rather dishevelled lady came to meet us, dancing in circles and babbling incoherently. O.C quietly told me "Don't worry Sue. She is not normal." There was absolutely no judgement in this – just a statement of fact. It made me think how unaccepting and insecure we are in our society.

On another occasion at a Kgotla meeting in Seronga a large crowd had gathered as there were some Government visitors. As I sat in the crowd I watched a very drunk man stagger in, making quite a lot of noise. One of the Customary Policemen walked over to him and started talking quietly to him. He took him by the hand and, whilst still whispering to him, led him away.

I couldn't help wondering how that scene would have played out in Australia. Perhaps a security guard would have tackled him to the ground, handcuffed him and called the police. It certainly wouldn't have been the calm, gentle solution I witnessed in Seronga.

One of our anti-hunting meetings was held in Gudigwa. Gudigwa is a bushman village with a strong history of hunting. We had made sure that they had been told we were coming but when we got there no-one was around. Good timekeeping is not a feature of life in Botswana but this was a totally deserted Kgotla – no Chief, no Customary Police, nobody.

Having travelled nearly 70kms on a sand road to get there, we thought it was worth waiting for people to be rounded up. Three hours later the meeting started. Discussion was lively with comic relief provided by Willie's old hunting tracker Patrick who seemed quite drunk. He kept dropping off to sleep and would wake up and shout "Kill all the elephants!"

O.C did have to point out to me afterwards that I should have accepted the offer of a snack on a cooked goat's head that one of the old men had brought with him in a small cooler box. Apparently it was an honour to be offered this delicacy. I had thought I was being polite declining so there was more for the others.

Trips to Maun

Trips to Maun always involved an early start.

One day I woke up and realised that I didn't have time to make tea so I gulped down a warm can of Fanta. I rushed to the boat station and sat bundled up in blankets for the motorboat trip along the Okavango River. When we reached Sepopa there was a bakkie waiting.

The chance of a lift to Sepopa Village instead of a 2km walk was appealing so I jumped on board and paid my two pula. Usually all journeys involved lots of waiting around but all connections fell into place that day. As we reached Sepopa Village a bus pulled up and we all got on. I knew that I needed to go to the toilet by this time but the next bus wouldn't be for hours.

After about an hour on the bus I knew I couldn't last another minute – I desperately needed to go to the toilet. As usual I was the only white person on the bus. I reluctantly approached the conductor and asked him if they could stop. The bus pulled over and everyone on the bus watched as I walked a little way off the road and then looked away politely as I crouched down behind a small bush to relieve myself. When I got back on the bus the conductor smiled at me and asked "Feel better now?" I guess I provided some entertainment that day. I was just glad I was wearing a long skirt.

We didn't always catch the bus. Many times we stood on the side of the main road and hitchhiked. With public transport being so scarce, most people would stop. This often involved clambering on the back of an open bakkie or truck. It was a hot, windy ride and as many people as possible were squashed in together but we were just happy to be on our way.

I spent a lot of time on buses, especially before we had our own vehicle. We needed a constant supply of cash to pay the polers. While it would have been easier to pay them once a month they really wanted payment at the end of each trip. So I regularly made the long trip to Maun by public transport and usually stayed in Maun one or two nights. I did banking, paid bills, shopped, visited Telekom, Council, Land Board and other places I needed to remind about our needs. It also gave me the opportunity to catch up with the safari companies that were sending us clients. I discovered Hilary's Coffee Shop and filled up on delicious fresh vegetables and salad.

At the bank I withdrew large amounts, sometimes 60,000 pula or more in small denominations as there often wasn't anywhere to change money in Seronga. Occasionally we could get change from the Co-op if they had plenty of money ready to send to their head office in Etsha 6. It was all about timing but they helped us when they could.

I had a blue crochet-type shoulder bag that I would cram the bundles of notes and bags of coins into. I would sit on the bus with the bag between my feet. I had no bad experiences doing this – more good luck than good planning I admit.

Speeding fines

On the way back from Francistown there were a lot of small settlements some of which only had four or five huts along the roadside but all of which had a 60km/hour speed limit. The open road limit in Botswana was 120km/hour so it was really annoying to have to slow down every few kilometres so, as usual, I was speeding along when I was pulled over by two policemen set up on the side of the road.

They were very polite and showed me the video of me rushing towards them at 140km/hr. After taking all my details and filling out the paperwork I was informed that the fine was 480 pula which I could pay at the police station in Maun if I wished.

I tried to charm my way out of the fine. I explained that I worked for a community organisation and that I had to travel all the way to Seronga. I said I couldn't afford to pay such a large fine as I had to buy diesel in Maun.

One policeman looked me in the eyes and then politely said "Madam, if you didn't drive so fast you wouldn't use so much diesel".

I couldn't argue with that and we eventually agreed on a 200pula fine which I paid to them and received a receipt.

Phil Potter from Sepopa Swamp Stop told me the story of how he was travelling from Sepopa to Maun when he was pulled over for speeding. He paid the fine but the policeman didn't have any change so he reluctantly had to overpay him 40pula.

A couple of weeks later he was travelling the same road and was pulled over again. He wasn't very happy as he had been careful not to speed this time. Imagine his surprise when the policeman walked up to him and said "Good morning Mr Potter. Here is your 40pula change."

Home in a hurry

My daughter was pregnant with her second child and I was fretting that I wouldn't be there for her when she had the baby. She was due in early May and I returned from my Christmas visit in January.

I discussed it with the Board and they were happy for me to return to Australia to be her. They completely understood as it was what would have happened in their families.

I contacted my son, David, and organised for him to pick me up at Sydney airport and drive me the one and a half hour hours to the Southern Highlands where El lives. I wanted to surprise her so she didn't know I was coming but was thrilled when I knocked on her door.

Nick was born on 1st May and I was able to meet him, spend a few days with them all before heading back to Botswana.

Guests

Our usual guests were backpackers travelling on overland trips around Africa. As we became more well-known small groups and individual backpackers or other budget travellers would come to experience an authentic African experience and to support a community owned business.

One day O.C. had gone to meet a plane arriving from Maun and when he got to the Camp came into the office and said "Sue, I really think you need to meet these people".

The group that had arrived were not like our usual travellers. They were very well dressed. The women wore a lot of jewellery and make-up and even had handbags. They had been told that they were coming on a fully catered day trip.

The Restaurant wasn't operating at that time and we had very little food. We quickly drove around the village collecting what we could find – bread, tinned meat, soft drinks, water. We drove the group out to the Mekoro station and gave them all a short ride on the mekoro, fed them the "picnic" we had hastily assembled, told them stories and then drove them back to fly out again. We did our best and the group understood our dilemma and at the end of the day I think they enjoyed the adventure.

On another occasion a small group of South Africans returned from their mekoro trip and asked to see me. They were not happy that the polers had only made one campfire and that they sat with the group while they ate. The South Africans felt that the polers were trying to make them feel guilty so they would share their food with them.

I had to try to explain that most of our visitors wanted the polers to join them at the campfire, that this was an important aspect of the whole experience. It was quite difficult to pass this feedback on to the polers as they were quite insulted.

For some reason the most difficult clients we had were Israelis. On a number of occasions groups of three or four Israelis would arrive and attempt to haggle over the price of the Mekoro trips. Often they were not on organised tours and would also negotiate with the boat drivers to get them to Seronga. One time they bargained hard with a boat driver to get a good price on the return trip up the river from Seronga to Sepopa and when they arrived, refused to pay. The boat driver was really upset and when he got back to Seronga came to me for help. As it had been a few hours since he left them and they were heading straight to the border, it was too late to get the police to intercept them. Such a shame when the boat driver was out of pocket for the fuel.

But on the whole, our guests arrived with open minds and a determination to enjoy the adventure. We provided budget trips and the opportunity to enjoy the Okavango Delta with the people who called it home.

Running Water

Whenever I could get to Gumare I would visit the Water Board office and ask about my application for a water tap at Moeletsi's house. One time when I went in there was only one person in the office.

"Where is everybody?" I asked. "They have gone to the cinema in Francistown" she answered.

I was surprised and asked "Have they all gone to the cinema? When will they be back?" "Yes" she answered "They have all gone. They should be back in about a week".

This didn't make sense so I kept probing and eventually realised that she actually meant seminar not cinema.

After I had moved into the Manager's House at the Camp I heard that the water Board was coming to install the tap and that I must rush to Gumare to pay them. I also had to purchase the hardware needed and was told that the Water Board would dig a trench and install the pipes to a point that was about 100 metres from Moeletsi's house. It was up to me to get a trench dug from that point to the house.

I hired three young men from the village and we negotiated a daily rate. After two days I went to check progress and found an unhappy group of diggers. They had been talking to the labourers who were working for the Water Board and had found out that these other diggers were being paid more than them and that when they had dug a certain length of trench they could stop for the day. They demanded the same conditions but I refused, reminding them that we had a fair deal. Their ringleader announced that they wouldn't do any more work and demanded that they be paid immediately for the two days.

Of course I didn't have the money with me so they refused to leave and climbed onto the land cruiser. No amount of discussion could move them so I drove to the Kgotla where I got the Customary Police and the Chief to mediate. I paid them the next day and one of them turned up to finish the job on his own so I was happy to give him a bonus.

After another few days we finally had a tap and running water but, like everyone else in the village that had a tap, we had to put a lock on it. Water was quite expensive and we would have been supplying water to everyone who lived nearby. I was no longer living in the house and I didn't want Moeletsi to end up with a huge water bill. I felt bad about this as I had personally experienced the daily challenge of fetching water.

And sometimes there was no water so someone would rush to the house of the "pumper" and get her to turn on the pump for the village. Sometimes this system failed and water had to be fetched from the river. Luckily the river water was fast flowing and clean and good to drink.

Work Permits

It took me quite a while to get around to applying for a Work Permit. For a time, when my three month tourist visa ran out, I would cross the border and re-enter Botswana with a new visa. This was a bit complicated by the fact that some of the staff at the Mohembo Botswana-Namibia border knew me as they sometimes visited Seronga to collect our VAT payments. This meant that I would need to travel even further, maybe into Zimbabwe and then back through a different border post.

While I was staying in Sareqo's house I joined a group that was going back to Ngepi in the Caprivi. I sorted out my visa and then travelled back to Seronga. I got off the motorboat and was making my way uphill from the Boat Station to the road when I saw Paul from Audi Camp driving down the road. He stopped.

"What are you doing here? I thought you had gone for good," he said.

"No." I replied "I just left to organise my visa. I am back to stay."

Paul gave me a lift back to Sareqo's compound but he wasn't very happy to see me. Almost as soon as I had left he had driven up to Seronga from Maun and moved into my house. A day or so later his girlfriend joined him. I don't think that they had asked Sareqo if they could stay in his daughter's house. I thought this was quite disrespectful. With their romantic interlude interrupted, they soon left

One other time I went all the way to Vic Falls and was able to get a lift back with a young guy who was driving back in a land cruiser that belonged to Pony Transport. It had been rented for an overland trip that ended in Vic Falls. It was all fitted out for safaris, complete with food.

We camped one night just off the road near Makgadikgadi Pans. I loved the rooftop tent which was easy to set up and which provided security against any animals in the area. We cooked over an open fire under the clear starry sky and then went to bed early, ready for the last leg of our journey.

Only 20kms from Maun we drifted to a stop as the vehicle ran out of fuel. The young driver eventually caught a bus to Maun, bought some fuel and then caught a bus back, leaving me to stay with the vehicle. After more than four hours we were on our way again. I was grateful to Tony and Denise from Pony Transport who had allowed me to hitch a ride back.

One evening near dusk I was driving a group of polers back from Xao after their return from a mekoro trip when we saw two sleek black 4x4s coming towards us. It was unusual to encounter any traffic on this road and I was ready to give them a friendly wave as we drove by. But they indicated that we should stop.

Both of the vehicles stopped and about five men got out. They asked me who I was and asked to see my passport. They explained that they had come to Seronga especially to check on me. I hummed and hawed a bit and said that my passport was with the lawyer in Francistown as I was applying for a Work Permit. They accepted this explanation and drove off.

I was so surprised! I suspected that someone had reported me to immigration. Probably in retaliation for thwarting their plans of having the Trust do whatever that person wanted. I had been able to advocate for the Trust on fairer rates of pay and had sourced funding, helping them towards independence.

I thought I had better sort out my Work Permit and put the wheels in motion. Part of the application included a certificate from a Doctor declaring that I was free from infectious diseases and was not insane. I wish I had kept a copy. I would have framed it and displayed in proudly on my wall.

To my surprise months later when I finally heard back, my application was declined. Luckily I had been dealing with quite a few Government officials over the time I was there and got a better result when an Assistant Minister supported my application.

I really understood how Botswana was trying to empower its own citizens by not giving Work Permits to foreigners for jobs that could be done by citizens but it was acknowledged that what I was doing, citizens weren't ready to do.

To get around the citizens first policy, many ex-pats in Botswana created understudy positions for citizens that came with time restrictions but allowed the ex-pats to stay to teach them the job. Another strategy seemed to be to make job descriptions so specific that no Motswana could meet the requirements. Jobs had to be advertised and some adverts said things like 'Must be fluent in English, German and French with at least two years' experience in camp management and a pilot's licence.' Well, maybe not that specific but very close.

The last straw

The polers were used to fitting as many people as possible on any vehicle and it was an ongoing battle to get them to understand that tourists had to be treated differently.

If we had a trip planned we would send a vehicle to drop polers at the Mekoro Station before the groups arrived. Some polers chose to camp at the Mekoro Station and wait for work.

When they arrived back from a trip into the Delta the guests would be transported first and an extra vehicle would be sent for the polers or the vehicle would return to get them after dropping off the guests. Guides that were going with the group and the Co-ordinator would travel with the group in the truck or land cruiser. There were usually about thirty-five people. If the polers went too this would have been about fifty-five people squashed on the truck. This wasn't considered crowded by local standards but would have been uncomfortable for our guests.

This created a constant battle with the polers who believed that because they owned the Trust they should be allowed to go on the vehicles whenever they wanted. It caused the final conflict that convinced me that it was time to move on.

I had told one of the Board Members that he couldn't go on the land cruiser. He dug his heels in and refused to get off. After a bit of a stand-off he got off the vehicle, continuing to argue with me. He then lifted both hands up, shoved me on the chest and I fell backwards onto the ground.

I completely understood that from a cultural point of view he had lost face by being told what to do by a woman but I also knew that I couldn't accept someone getting physical with me. I went with the driver and some of the other polers who had witnessed the incident to the Police. When we got there they suddenly clammed up and said that they hadn't actually seen anything. They couldn't afford to take my side against one of their own.

I felt that this was the last straw and decided that I couldn't do it anymore.

Looking back on this incident, I have come to realise that I was probably ready to move on. Once the Camp was built and the business operating successfully it had become clear that the Trust might never be able to run it by themselves. I realised that I had begun to feel a bit trapped.

I moved out that day and went to Maun.

Maun

In Maun I arranged to stay in a house owned by Jimmi and Heidi who I had met when they brought groups to Seronga but who were usually based in Namibia. I set up my house so that Trust members could stay with me when they came to Maun and continued to liaise with safari companies and organise supplies for Mbiroba, driving the loaded Daihatsu to Sepopa to transfer supplies to our motorboat.

Life in Maun was so different to life in Seronga. There was a large expat population that was generally divided by culture or occupation. Afrikaans or Dutch heritage South Africans largely socialised with each other while English heritage South Africans seemed to mix with everyone. There were also a lot of pilots from Australia and New Zealand and of course safari company employees came from all over the world and were often young and adventurous. A lot of the strong Indian community ran small businesses.

Houses, furniture and cars were usually sold on when people left so it was common to visit "the house that so and so built" or sit on the lounge that "such and such used to own".

Because everyone was so far from home and the population was fluid, newcomers were welcomed and there was always a braai (BBQ) or trip up the river happening. I especially enjoyed lazy Sunday afternoons on the river with Hillary, Ron, Pierre, Desiree, Monica and Christiana. We would motor upriver against the current and then tie up for drinks and snacks. Or we would just drift back down the river chatting, eating and drinking.

Those who had been there a long time, many of whom had become Botswana citizens, often owned more than one property and business. There were a few western style restaurants, a couple of supermarkets, a gym and classes in everything ranging from Setswana language classes to belly dancing classes. Other support businesses flourished as expats needed work permits, business registrations and assistance navigating the ever changing Botswana rules and regulations.

I made some good friends and enjoyed having the support of people who shared a western background. I learnt some great South African expressions. When told that something would happen *now* meant that it would happen sometime in the future. *Just now* meant soon and *now-now* meant immediately.

I learnt that you could always *"make a plan"* and that the sympathetic term *"shame"* covered everything from a paper cut to a plane crash.

I found most South Africans to be generous, resourceful and to generally share the same sense of humour as Australians.

Security became an issue for the first time as the distance between the haves and have nots became so obvious. Expats lived in proper houses, drove good cars and always seemed to have plenty of disposable income. Many of the locals did not. I learned to always lock houses and cars.

The police were under-resourced and so a 911 Neighbourhood Watch Network developed.

Residents paid an annual membership fee and each household had a radio to use to request help in an emergency or to respond to calls for assistance. Many thieves were quickly tracked back to their homes where they could be apprehended by police. If a call for help went out, people in vehicles and on foot would arrive within minutes.

While I was staying at Jimmi and Heidi's house I had a burglary and lost my much loved Nikon camera. This was especially annoying as I knew it would be sold for a pittance but had been very expensive and was my present to myself when I sold my

Dive Shop. The only compensation I had was wishing I could see the look on the thieves' faces when they unpacked the neatly folded khaki pants they had stolen from me. Far from being useful men's pants they were only ¾ pants suitable for my short stature. I am sure they were surprised!

With the Camp so busy, we were constantly driving to Maun for supplies, leaving the Camp without the land cruiser for two or three days at a time. When I heard about the opportunity to get good quality used vehicles donated from Japan I discussed it with the Board and we jumped at the chance. As we were a community organisation the vehicle was free but we did have to pay freight costs and we didn't have a lot of say in what vehicle we would receive. We outlined what we needed and after a couple of months the vehicle was delivered to Gaborone.

Rupes and I made another trip from Seronga to Gaborone to sort out customs and take delivery.

The "truck" we received was a small Daihatsu with the smallest wheels I had ever seen. It was obviously not going to be able to handle sand or water so the plan was to use it on the tarred road only, buying supplies in Maun and then delivering them to Sepopa where they would be taken by motorboat to Seronga. But I wanted the Trust to see what we had paid for so at the end of the wet season when the road was fairly firm between Mohembo and Seronga, we set off.

The journey went slowly but well until we got about 20kms from Seronga where we ground to a halt with the bottom of the truck balancing on the ridge between the tracks on the road.

We pushed it and pulled it but it wouldn't budge. Luckily an army truck going in the opposite direction stopped, the soldiers jumped off, picked up the little Daihatsu and set in on a smoother part of the track. With quick thanks from us, they jumped back on their truck and drove off.

We realised that the Daihatsu couldn't spend much time in Seronga as the road was only going to get softer as the dry season progressed.

Later, Rupes and I travelled from Maun through the Kalahari and over the border into Namibia so we could visit all the Namibian based safari companies and all the camps and lodges on the way to Botswana. It was important that these places had information on the OPT and our affordable mekoro safaris. Otherwise they would only have directed all travellers to the trips operating out of Maun.

We stayed with Jimmi and Heidi in Windhoek and then travelled on to the coast. This was the first time Rupes had seen the ocean and he was amazed at its size. When I asked him to pose for a photo on the beach with the calm sea in the background he wondered "Is it safe? Are there no crocodiles?"

After visiting all the safari companies, we made a trip to the aquarium where the inquisitive sting rays held Rupes spellbound. He also had the chance to ride a quad bike over the huge sand dunes so it was a trip of many firsts for him.

I travelled to Seronga every three or four weeks but the Trust understandably decided that they wanted their Manager on-site. OC stepped up as Manager and stayed on for a while but eventually left out of frustration. He could no longer refer difficult decisions to me and really felt the pressure from the other polers – especially the Board. He went to work as a guide at Wilderness Safaris.

By now I had moved into the house in Sedia built by Steve and Sarah from Phakawe Safaris. I knew them well from their visits to Seronga with groups and they were always welcoming and hospitable when I visited Maun. It was their computer I had borrowed to do funding applications and I had enjoyed watching their house being built and furnished. It was a real house with a proper bathroom and kitchen. It was set back from the road and surrounded by a wire and lethaka (reed) fence. On the property were also a two roomed building, a thatched rondavel, an outside bathroom and a large carport.

Steve and Sarah were parting ways. Sarah had lived through a terrible experience where she was attacked at home by robbers wanting her to open the wall safe set in the brick wall in their bedroom. When she refused they beat her about the head and she ended up in hospital. Steve had been away on safari at the time. On his return they fitted alarms, sturdy security doors and window bars made of reinforcing iron so their house was now super secure.

They both intended to leave Botswana and I talked to them about buying their house. I wanted to be settled in Botswana and I loved the idea of living in a real house after over four years living in tents and huts without even running water. I started by renting their house and when I returned to Australia at the end of the year, arranged a mortgage on my Australian house and bought the house in Sedia. I was so happy to have my own house.

I rented the two roomed building and the carport to Mac, a South African mechanic to use as a workshop. I used the rondavel as my office. I had running water, electricity and a telephone. What luxury!

One night I had been to Island Safaris to have dinner with Marilyn. I was driving the Daihatsu and as I turned onto the main road from the Island Safari turnoff, two vehicles came speeding down the otherwise deserted road towards me. One slowed down behind me and the other pulled in front of me. I had heard that this was a common car-jacking move in South Africa, so I swerved around the front vehicle and drove around him on the shoulder of the road.

Ahead of me I could see the entrance to the Sports Bar where I knew there would be a lot of people. I drove as fast as I could and pulled into the entrance and into the car park. I thought that would be the end of it. Surely they wouldn't follow me in to this busy place! But they did.

I screeched to a halt in the middle of the crowded car park, locked my doors and started leaning on the horn. The two black South African men leapt from the vehicles and were banging on the door and window, they bent the windscreen wipers and kept screaming that I had cut them off and they were going to teach me a lesson.

I was really panicked and just kept leaning on the horn. Some local people came out of the kitchen to see what was happening but in typical Batswana fashion, didn't want to get involved and just kept watching. Finally the Manager of the Sports Bar came out and chased the two guys off by saying he had called the police.

I was really shaken and too nervous to go home alone in case they were waiting for me or followed me. So I drove back to Island Safaris and we called the police from there. The police came quickly. They interviewed all the witnesses and took statements. But nothing came of it, as usual.

Conservation International

While working with OPT I had met Sharon Safran and other employees of Conservation International (CI) who were working with the Bukakhwe Cultural Conservation Trust(BCCT) in Gudigwa. Whenever we met Sharon and I talked a lot about the challenges of working in remote areas with community groups and we compared notes about our experiences. When Sharon returned home to the USA she recommended that I be employed to replace her as a consultant on the Bushman Traditional Village project.

Gudigwa was an artificial settlement built around guaranteed water supply and a new school. Although all of the same ethnic background (Bukakhwe/San/Bushman/Basarwa – all different names for the same people) the village was made up of nine separate clans. These clans would normally have been nomadic, happy to meet occasionally and even inter-marry but forced together in this permanent settlement there were often conflicts. These conflicts spilled over into the camp.

Many of the Camp employees were from the same family or clan. This might have been partly because this family encouraged their members to get a good education but it was hard not to question how much nepotism was involved. Three of the four guides were brothers, with different mothers but the same father. While they understood and accepted that personal conflicts were unacceptable in the camp, there was one incident that underlined the tension that was always just under the surface. One of the brothers had got another in trouble at the camp so the aggrieved brother waited until they were off duty. He then got his revenge by lying in wait in the village to beat him with a heavy piece of wood as he walked by. Another of the brothers had been dismissed from another camp for attacking the Manager with a knife.

I found that the Bukakhwe that I met lived with their emotions just below the surface. When they were happy or excited they jumped around, laughing and talking rapidly. Similarly, if they were unhappy about something you would be left in no doubt as to how they were feeling. They were also clever and quick to learn.

Gudigwa Camp was developed by BCCT in partnership with CI and Wilderness Safaris. Guests were booked by Wilderness Safaris and flew in from other Wilderness Safaris' camps. The idea was to provide a one night experience.

Located five kms from the village, the Camp could accommodate up to sixteen guests in large grass huts modelled on traditional bushman shelters but with the comfort of full outdoor bathrooms with hot showers and flushing toilets.

Guests would have a guided bush walk when they arrived in the afternoon and in the evening community members would arrive from the village and don traditional clothing. The women would sit with adorable small children dressed in traditional skins and feeding babies and demonstrate the making of necklaces and other decorative items out of ostrich egg shell. The men would demonstrate how to make fire by rubbing two sticks together and how to make traditional hunting aids such as bows and arrows. Guests were encouraged to ask questions and try the crafts themselves. There were photo opportunities galore.

Welcome drinks were served in ostrich eggs and at Gudigwa Camp we always offered the guests interesting bar snacks such as spicy nuts and dried mopane worms. We encouraged them to try the worms as they were such a novelty and I would always recommend them heartily. I have to admit, though, that in all the years I was in Botswana I never ate mopane worms, or the also popular flying termites.

The guides led the story telling. They talked about their traditional lifestyle, explaining what life was like when they led a nomadic existence. They explained how hunting parties would chase down large game like giraffes, shooting them with poisonous arrows. The giraffes didn't die immediately so the men would have to keep following the poisoned animal until it eventually expired. They would then butcher and eat as much as they could whilst sending for the rest of the clan to join them and enjoy the feast.

There was inter-marrying between the clans. Sometimes even unborn children were pledged in marriage. Brides would join their husband's clan when still very young children so they could get used to their new clan's way of doing things.

The guides also explained why the Bukakhwe dance the way they do.

A long time ago three men were taken to meet the creator who asked them what special talents they would like.

The first was an Indian. He said he would like to be a good businessman and the creator granted this wish. That is why so many businesses are run by Indians.

The second man was an Englishman. He asked the creator to make him a good engineer and the creator granted his wish. That is why the Englishmen had invented things like the aeroplane.

The creator then turned to the Bukakhwe man who was so shy and overwhelmed at being in front of the creator that he just stood on the spot unmoving. He was so nervous that he began shaking all over. The Creator had to guess what the Bukakhwe wanted and watching how he moved, he told him that from then on the Bukakhwe would be great dancers. They would dance without moving their feet, from the waist up. That is why the Bukakhwe dance the way they do.

The staff working at the dinners couldn't resist the pull of the dance and would always join in dancing with the other villagers who were dressed in traditional skins.

Delicious dinners were prepared by the Wilderness Safaris-trained cooks and the bar was usually kept busy until the day's early start and exciting game drives caught up with the guests. Because of the large numbers of lions and elephants in the area, all guests were escorted back to their tent by a guide.

Early the next morning the guests would have a quick snack and then head out on a guided walk with traditionally dressed villagers and a guide. During the walk they would be shown plants used for medicine, bush food, and how to find underground water. Tracks in the sand were examined and the guide explained what animals had been past and how long ago.

The walk would culminate in a clearing where a full cooked breakfast would be served. Later that morning the guests would fly on to their next destination.

By the time I got involved with the project building work on the Camp was well under way. After a period as a Consultant on the project, I was offered the job as Ecotourism Officer at CI. We hired a Manager and the Camp opened.

Unfortunately the Manager left suddenly in the middle of the busy season and I had to step in to act as Manager. Most camps in the Delta are run by couples. Having a couple supplies a broader range of skills and experience and they are there to support each other. The Manager at Gudigwa was a young, single woman. She had to face many challenges on her own and found it very hard.

The Gudigwa Bushmen aren't the typically small, wizened up Bushmen of the Gods Must be Crazy fame. They are river Bushmen or Bukakhwe. Many of the old people still look like the stereotypical Bushmen but the younger generation are much larger and taller. Our head guide, Zero, was over six feet tall.

Conservation International was asked to work with the people of Gudigwa Village to help them develop an income–generating project. It was decided to design, build and run a Bushman Traditional Village as a tourism enterprise. A relationship was developed with Okavango Wilderness Safaris who already employed many locals in their safari camps.

Lets was one of the Assistant Managers at Gudigwa Camp. He told me how he received the scars on his head. Before Gudigwa had its own school, the children of the village were sent to the nearby village of Beetsha – twenty-six kilometres away. They had to stay in Beetsha as it was too far and too dangerous to travel on foot each day. Most were very homesick and unhappy. Many would run away and go home.

Although the Bukakhwe traditionally have a good relationship with the Bayei who live in the area, there is a history of Bushmen being treated harshly by other Batswana. In the past they were regarded as slaves by the other tribes and even today can often be found doing cattle minding and menial jobs for little or no money.

At Beetsha the children had to board at the school as most had no relations in this village. The accommodation they shared was a large canvas tent with no sides.

One night Lets awoke to what he thought was a dog attacking him. It had him by the head and was pulling him backwards out of the tent, away from the other children. He kept struggling and called out to wake up the others. They realised that it was in fact a lion that had the nine-year old boy by the head and they shouted and hit at it. The lion ran away.

Elephants and lions

The water system of the Okavango Delta is constantly changing as the plates of the earth move. Gudigwa used to have a large river and the village is built alongside the riverbed but when I was first there, Gudigwa was dry and dusty and many of the children had never seen water in the riverbed.

As part of the Gudigwa Camp project we laid pipes to an old water hole and pumped water into it daily. This was done to attract wildlife back into the area around the camp. At first two elephants starting visiting it each evening in the dry season. Then word must have spread and more and more started arriving. Some nights we had more than twenty elephants at the 20 foot diameter water hole. They were really obliging and would arrive as the Bukakhwe sat around the campfire telling stories to the tourists that had flown in that day.

The amusing part was seeing the Bukakhwe reacting with concern and suspicion whilst the tourists (who had probably already been to a lot of game parks) had begun to think that Africa is just one big show and we found we had to watch them closely to make sure they didn't get too close in their endeavours to get "that" photo.

Most of the elephants that visited were males but occasionally we would have the delight of a breeding herd visiting – all females and often with babies. It was always exciting.

There were no fences at the camp and during the safety briefing on arrival the guests were always told not to walk anywhere without one of the staff because of the constant danger of lions and elephants but regularly the alert went out that a tourist was wandering out of the camp during their rest time and one of the guides would rush off to intercept them.

One night we were kept awake by extra loud trumpeting of elephants, answered by the loud roaring of lions. It went on for literally hours and was too loud to ignore. The next day the guides checked all the tracks and worked out that the lions were trying to get to the waterhole but that the elephants wouldn't let them. In desperation the lions had found our water pump that was fed by well-points deep in the ground and had chewed through the 50mm polythene pipes to get to the water.

Once they got used to people being around at the camp, a bachelor herd of seven young male elephants decided that the trees around the camp made a nice home. Sometimes we would be stuck in the kitchen for hours as we were surrounded by elephants and couldn't come out. I realised that the Bushmen had survived so well because of the respect they paid the elephants. They would do anything to avoid an encounter with elephants.

The Manager's house at Gudigwa Camp was situated about fifty metres from the nearest inhabited building which was the Assistant Managers' house. Once all the guests had been escorted to their huts and the waiters and Assistant Managers had gone to bed, I had to negotiate my way in the dark along a narrow track in the high grass to my house. The staff always kindly warned me to be careful of elephants but they didn't offer to walk me to my house.

In fact, at a time when we were worried about lions around and in the camp at night, the barman and I were the last ones up and he asked me to walk him to the staff village. It was only when I was walking back alone in the pitch dark with only a small torch that I wondered why I, a foreign woman alone, was thought to be able to look after myself but these much more bush-savvy and experienced bushmen needed to be walked home. I guess I was the Manager so they thought I didn't need looking after. The next morning there were lion prints all around my house and up and down my path – exactly where I had walked the night before.

One night I woke in the isolated Manager's house to a really loud grinding noise. It took a few seconds to realise that it was the sound of elephants chewing right outside my window.

The first night I was thrilled. Wow, here I was in Africa in my bed looking at an elephant only three feet from me. After a while I decided that since I was awake I would go to the toilet. The bathroom was en-suite in that it was connected by a door to the house but it was completely outside with just a reed fence around it. There was a toilet and a shower- both completely open and uncovered.

As I opened the door to go outside I saw a really huge elephant head looking over the fence at me. I decided that I didn't really need to go to the toilet. Back inside I thought about how flimsy my mud house with a grass roof was and spent quite a while wondering what I would do if one of these huge bull elephants decided to lean on it or if they dropped a branch through the thatched roof.

It was an exciting night spent admiring the elephants through the window – their amazingly versatile trunks, their beautiful eyelashes and the funny tough hairs on their skin. They walked around so quietly – the only sound was leaves being ripped from the trees, tufts of grass being dexterously pulled up by the trunk and fed into the mouth, strong teeth grinding away at the food and the crunch of branches being ripped off the trees.

The second night I also awoke for a while but after admiring my large visitors I went back to sleep. By the fifth night of broken sleep it had changed from "oh wow, elephants" to "oh damn, elephants again" The novelty had worn off.

Confrontation

We had tried to introduce some slightly different practices. In most Camps workers were trucked in and stayed for two to three months, being provided with rations during their stay.

Because Gudigwa Village was only 5kms away, workers were able to return home if there was a gap between guests. We started by giving them rations but found it was much more efficient to provide meals instead as they took the rations home between guest bookings and were then left with no food when they returned. We had three cooks and we rostered them to take turns to cook staff meals. This wasn't popular with the cooks who felt it was a step down to cook for the other workers. One cook in particular had a problem with this and with everything else she was asked to do. I cut her some slack as I was aware that the previous year she had been in the Camp during construction and her baby had died but it got to the point that her behaviour couldn't continue.

The Camp was owned by the BCCT which was managed by a Board of Trustees. Any issue with a staff member was taken to the Board and their advice sought. After a lot of issues with this cook the Board had decided that if there was one more issue, she should be fired. This decision was conveyed to her by the Board. The day came when she once again refused to do what she was asked. I requested that she come with me into the village to meet with the Chairman of the Board. She refused to go so I went with one of the Assistant Managers. On hearing what had happened, the Chairman agreed that we had no alternative but to fire her. I returned to the Camp and told her of the decision. She refused to accept it.

At the time a young American intern called Todd had just arrived to work on the project for six months. Todd had been contracted before Sharon left and I had been present at his phone interview where it was made really clear that he would receive only a small payment per month to help with living expenses. As I was now based in the Camp waiting to recruit a new Manager, he joined me there.

On that day we sat in the area behind the kitchen and ate lunch together. The cook was following me everywhere. In her hand she carried a wooden axe handle which she periodically slapped onto her palm in a threatening manner. I ignored her and kept talking to Todd. As I stood up and began to walk back to the kitchen with my empty plate, she poked me hard between the shoulder blades with the end of the axe handle. I spun around on reflex.

Unfortunately she was standing so close that my empty plate poked her in her pregnant stomach and she called out that I was hurting her baby. She immediately started to smash me across my shoulders, arms and back with the axe handle. I tried to get away into the office and Todd asked her to hand over the axe handle, which she did. She then grabbed a large knife from the kitchen, stripped a branch from a tree and whittled a spear from it. All this time she was yelling abuse at me and threatening to kill me.

The two Assistant Managers joined me in the office and we discussed what we could do. They tried to calm her down by talking to her but she was beyond reasoning. They sent the vehicle off to the Village to fetch the Chairman and other Board members and we decided that we would have to cancel the group that were soon due to arrive from another Camp because we couldn't guarantee their safety. This involved talking almost in code to the radio operator at Wilderness Safaris so he would understand the seriousness of what was happening without ruining the reputation of the project.

Some Board members arrived and conducted a hearing. They agreed that I had acted according to their instructions but were more concerned that I had cancelled the guests. They were angry about the lost revenue. Even though the Assistant Managers had agreed that the situation was serious enough that we had to cancel the guests, when faced with their fellow villagers they became silent and refused to defend our decision.

It was agreed that I should go to the Police and report the assault. Of course nothing really came of the complaint but the policeman was very sympathetic, telling me that just the previous month he had been chased through the village by someone with a spear.

I was bruised across my back, shoulders and arms. I was incredibly lucky that she didn't hit my head as the damage would have been so much worse. I was really shaken but managed to keep it all together even though I was clearly in shock. We arranged to return to Maun, leaving a skeleton crew behind to look after the Camp. Mike at Wilderness Safaris and Lovemore at CI were very supportive and it was decided that as it was close to the end of the season, the camp would remain closed.

Looking back on this incident, I am surprised that I wasn't offered counselling – especially with CI being an American organisation. Because I was willing to "soldier on", I just kept working on the project.

As Todd had just arrived, I invited him to stay temporarily at my house. He soon settled in to the expat life. There were always a lot of young pilots and safari staff around ready to party. He quickly also bonded with another young CI staff member and they were out most nights.

Having Todd around at work and at home had become annoying. He was a nice enough guy but we had little in common. In his naivety he had suggested to Lovemore that if he was able to go back to Gudigwa he could have a drink at the bar and play some soccer in the village to sort out all our problems up there. At this stage he had been in the country only a few weeks and had spent only four days in Gudigwa. All of his socialising was done with expats and I think he had no real understanding of the culture or the underlying problems at Gudigwa. I really wanted him to move out but had got myself into that uncomfortable situation where I couldn't bring myself to just ask him to leave. In this situation it always seems like you should just tell a person but I really dislike confrontation and just felt more and more stressed about it. Luckily after three months he announced that he was moving in with a friend.

He also hadn't endeared himself at work as he had complained that he wasn't earning enough money. He had enlisted the support of his friend at CI but was reminded that he had agreed to the terms of his internship before arriving. He finished with CI soon after and volunteered for very short times on a few other projects around the Delta.

We received word that the Camp had completely burnt down. Wildfires were not uncommon in the Delta but it seemed really suspicious that Gudigwa Camp had burnt down when the caretaker had left on a shopping trip to the next village.

The destruction was complete with even the underground plastic septic tanks becoming molten messes. It was decided to relocate the camp and just bury the debris. I wasn't sure how that gelled with the conservation aspects but we did as asked. It was then my job to rebuild the Camp.

I must say that with the support and resources of Wilderness Safaris this was an easier process than when I had organised the building of Mbiroba Camp. Most of the furniture and supplies were sourced from South Africa and trucked in across the Delta. We had a disappointing experience with the first camp when a truck load of beds, bedding etc had been lost when the truck transporting it had caught on fire. We learnt that there is no such thing as insurance on goods being trucked in. But rebuilding and restocking this time went without incident.

My Dad

While I was working for CI I received a call from my family to tell me that my father was critically ill in New Zealand. I took some time off and flew to New Zealand. My flight stopped off in Sydney on the way so I arranged to meet up with El, Dave and their partners at a hotel close to the airport. I only had a few hours but I really wanted to see them.

Once I arrived in New Zealand I had an internal flight to Hastings and arrived desperately hoping that I wasn't too late to say goodbye to my Dad. I made it in time. Dad had been given a blood transfusion the day before and had rallied around. I stayed with my sister and spent each day at the hospital. I saw Dad decline. He spent a lot of his time sleeping and I sat beside his bed reading. My father had a really challenging upbringing and found it hard to express his feelings although we often teased him as he teared up watching something sad on TV. I remember that as a child when I hugged him he would remain almost unbending in the hug.

He was very restless one day at the hospital and admitted that his feet were sore. His kidneys were shutting down and the circulation to his feet was obviously faltering. I convinced him to let me give him a foot massage. He didn't complain and the next day asked me to do it again. It then became a request five or six times a day. I believe he enjoyed the relief but I also like to think he was enjoying the contact. When a nurse asked if he wanted her to help him shave he answered "No. My daughter will do it".

While I was staying at my sister's I got a call from a friend of hers who was in a book club. They were reading Alexander McCall Smith's First Lady's Detective Agency, set in Botswana, and wanted to ask me about living in Botswana. I told her that I related to how the Batswana in the book thought and acted – based on my time in Seronga.

A couple of years later I was surprised when an English expat friend expressed her annoyance at how unrealistic and unbelievable these books were. I realised that her interactions with Batswana were in a town setting or as employees in a safari camp. I knew that life in the villages was quite different. When I lived in the village I had to walk everywhere so I mixed with the villagers. This would change after the Trust bought the Land cruiser and the Board suggested I could use it to travel back and forth to work but I also spent a lot of time with Rupes' family and friends.

I remember hearing some expats complaining one day that one of their staff members had left to attend their grandmother's funeral AGAIN. Maybe they didn't understand that in Botswana aunts are often referred to as and treated as grandmothers. Often they have as much influence on a person's life decisions as the parents do. With our restricted definition of grandmother these expats thought their employee was taking advantage of them.

Through my work I had contact with many people who had no experience of town living and I had to learn how they viewed things and make sure I spent time on traditional greetings, asked about their families and how they were before I got to the core of what I wanted. If a worker was sick and wanted to leave work, I had to spell out whether they would be paid or not. My agreeing they should go home could be interpreted as meaning that they could leave, stay away a while and still be paid. This wasn't always the situation.

I learnt never to take anything for granted although I admit to making some assumptions in the early days that led to misunderstandings. O.C and Rupes became my guides to village life, making sure I didn't accidentally offend someone.

I had organised to stay in New Zealand for nine days and then had to return to South Africa for some important CI meetings so I sadly farewelled my Dad and my family, knowing that this would be the last time I saw my father. I felt terrible when I left for the long journey back to Africa and when I landed I heard that my father had died while I was on the flight. I was so grateful for the chance to spend some time with him and treasure the closeness we developed. When something goes wrong, you realise just how far away you are living.

Film Crew

I had arranged for a film crew to come to Gudigwa to promote the project and unfortunately this occurred during a visit from CI Head Office staff from the U.S. I worked until after 10pm each night to try to cover everything before I had to leave but still felt that the CI people were not happy when I left to travel to Gudigwa but I felt that I had made a commitment to the people at Gudigwa and that came first.

The filming went well with the guides and other villagers all dressed in traditional skins and demonstrating how to track animals, how to find food, make fire etc.

We were all camping in the bush as the new camp was still being rebuilt. The film crew laid out a tarpaulin with all their cameras and equipment on it. They asked me if it was safe to leave it all there overnight. Erring on the side of caution, I suggested that perhaps they should put it away at night. I was worried that animals might come in the night and damage or steal the equipment.

The next day I noticed that the community members were a little cool towards me. I wasn't sure why and as I had to have all my questions translated, couldn't find out. Much later I found that one of the Assistant Managers had told them that I had told the film crew that the villagers couldn't be trusted and that they should put their equipment in their tent at night. So frustrating!

Once again I was the victim of this Assistant Manager's hidden agenda. He was always friendly and polite to my face but it turned out that behind my back he was constantly criticising and undermining me. It was impossible to counter this sabotage as I usually wasn't aware of what he had said. He was one of the ones who denied being part of the decision making about closing the camp earlier and he was the one who beat up his brother. He was also the person supposed to be on duty when the camp burnt down.

Once Gudigwa Camp was up and running again we hired a new Manager and I decided to work for myself as a consultant. I registered my company, Anther Enterprises, and began working for other community organisations. Some of the projects such as helping the Sexaxa Community register a Trust were unpaid but I was happy to use the experience I had gained to help other communities. I was conscious that lots of white safari companies and businesses were coming into the Delta and it was hard for communities to protect their own interests.

Expat Life

I finally bought a car for myself. The white Toyota dual cab was perfect for work and for weekends away. I was finally going to be able to explore the rest of Botswana. While I was in Seronga I worked seven days a week for eleven months of the year and then went home to Australia for a month each year. There were so many places I wanted to visit and now that I was living in Maun I might have the opportunity.

When the Camp Manager quit without warning, I had to rush to Gudigwa. I was running a bit late so I got one of Mac's mechanics to drive me to the airport and then asked him to leave the keys with Rupes. When I flew back in for a meeting at CI, I met a friend at the airport who mentioned that he thought he had seen my wrecked car outside the Police Station. Sure enough Rupes had decided to take the dual cab to the liquor store. He didn't have a licence, had little driving experience and had been drinking so the inevitable result was that he rolled it. The vehicle was completely written off and I was only able to get a small amount for it as parts.

I was disappointed and furious. After a huge row Rupes moved back to Seronga but after a few weeks he returned. Despite all the challenges he presented me with, he was loving and funny.

I joined the book club which included women from all over the expat community, including a number of lovely Indian women. There was always a good turnout when they hosted book club as we got to enjoy delicious Indian snacks. There wasn't a lot of intellectual discussion about books at book club but there was fun and good company and the chance to swap books.

When I was in Seronga I used to buy second hand books from one of the safari companies every time I went to Maun and would fill my backpack with as many books as I could fit. I used to swap them sometimes with one of the policemen who liked reading. The Book Club was like a treasure trove with boxes and boxes of books available. I also enjoyed meeting new people, having a wine and a chat.

Sexaxa is a small settlement on the road between Maun and Moremi Game Reserve. They had set up a small traditional village where they could demonstrate traditional crafts and sell baskets. Because the settlement wasn't gazetted as a village they weren't able to register their Trust but wanted all paperwork ready in case their situation changed. I was impressed with how organised they were.

I was also able to use the experience I had gained to co-author a CBNRM paper on Labour Laws in Botswana. This was in conjunction with Kutlwano Modiakgotla a citizen who was previously a District Labour Officer and was then working as a private consultant in Maun – assisting with company formation, obtaining work and residence permits and trading licences.

The paper was entitled *Labour Laws and Community Based Organisations in Botswana*. In it we tried to explain the Labour Laws in a practical way for community organisations using real life examples and including three case studies. I was able to draw on my recent work with the BCCT in Gudigwa and the Okavango Community –Trust (OCT) in Seronga. I was also asked to include the Gaing-o Community Trust. These three Trusts were chosen to cover different approaches and different situations. The BCCT had received NGO and consultant assistance to formulate their labour policies. The OCT was selected as an example of an older Trust with a joint venture partner. The Gaing-O Community Trust was trying to become more professional and was undergoing a lot of labour changes.

My son David and his partner Samantha had arrived to visit and to help me celebrate my 50th birthday and I invited them along on my research trip.

The Gaing-o Community Trust is located in Mmatshumo Village, 25kms from Letlhakane in the closest village to Kubu Island. The Trust operated two campsites at Lekhubu (Kubu Island).

The community consisted of 900 people, mostly spread over a large area. There was no wildlife in the area and their partnership was with the National Museum of Botswana, for whom they act as custodians of the island which is a national monument. The entrance and camping fees charged to visitors were used to cover part of the running costs of the Trust and to look after the island. The Trust was hoping to get funding to build a Lodge.

They had some labour problems in the past when they changed the jobs of caretaker to field guides. They had a General Manager and Project Advisor funded by DED (German Development Services) but had just selected a General Manager and an understudy to help move the Trust towards independence.

It was nearly 400kms from Maun to Mmatshumo Village and we set off early. Poor Samantha. She had never even been on a camping holiday before and never had to squat on the side of the road to answer nature's call. She elected to hold on until we got to the village where she was horrified to find that the only long drop toilet was very neglected with a broken door and toilet seat and it was VERY smelly. Much nicer to squat behind a bush on the side of the road.

Dave and Sam had previously enjoyed a mokoro safari with the OPT and then drove to meet me at Gudigwa Camp so they had seen my two previous projects. I was so pleased that they would have some understanding of my life in Botswana and appreciate the satisfaction I received from being able to help people achieve independence and improve their standards of living.

We later did a road trip to Zimbabwe and did some touristy things including my adventurous son bungee jumping twice. We went to Zambia and did a helicopter tour over Victoria Falls and we bought some great wooden carvings.

Tourists were still using Zimbabwe dollars at that time and I can't remember the exchange rate but I do remember that when we changed money we took along a backpack for the bundles and bundles of notes.

On a night out at a nice hotel we ate so many different animals that Sami commented that the only animal left to eat was the Pudu. (The last remaining population of Pudu antelope consists of only 200 animals and we had seen them in Chobe.)

We thought it was screamingly funny when it was time to pay the bill and we had to ask for a tray to stack all the notes on. But then we thought lots of things were screamingly funny on that trip.

Whilst still in Maun we had experienced the ugly prehistoric looking armoured crickets. They had arrived in almost plague proportions and I was really creeped out by them. They reminded me of wetas that are found in New Zealand and which my mother had always told me would bite me if I touched them. I don't think that wetas really bite but I was very nervous of them.

One year at the end of my Christmas break in Australia I stayed the last night at home with Dave and Sami. I didn't feel at all well and, not being able to breathe well, didn't get much sleep.

On the way to catch my flight back to Africa, I was obviously not well but insisted I was fine. On the plane for the first and only time in my life I actually had a whole row of three seats to myself and thought how good it would be to be able to lie down during the 17 hour flight. I soon discovered that if I did lie down I struggled to breathe so I ended up sitting up the whole flight.

I usually overnighted in Johannesburg to catch a flight to Botswana the next afternoon so I went to my hotel. I felt really bad by this time so asked for directions to the nearest chemist and set off to see what they could give me. The pharmacist took one look at me and refused to sell me anything. He told me that there was a medical centre in the same street and insisted I go there to see a Doctor. The Doctor sent me for chest x-rays which showed that I had pneumonia. He said I should be hospitalised but that he wouldn't recommend any of the local hospitals. He gave me antibiotics and painkillers and I went back to the hotel.

I told reception that I was sick and wouldn't be checking out the next day. Over the next three days I slept, took medicine and slept some more. As soon as I was well enough I booked my flight to Maun. It took me over six weeks before I had my usual energy back and looking back, I found the whole incident quite scary.

Another year I thought it would be good if Rupes met me in Johannesburg when I returned from Australia. He had never been to South Africa and I thought we could at least have a quick look around Jo'burg.

Once again I wasn't well when I arrived so I went straight to my room and had a sleep without putting my passport and money in the hotel safe as I would normally have done.

Rupes arrived from Botswana a few hours later and we decided to walk to a nearby shopping centre to see a Doctor there. We were only about 100 metres from the hotel entrance when a car drove quickly down the street and drew to a halt beside us. Three men got out, they flashed ID badges and said they were police and demanded to inspect my bag and Rupes' pockets and wallet. They were talking a lot, asking Rupes who he was, where he was from and whether he had any marijuana. They made him turn out his pockets and open up his wallet.

When they got to my bag they came across my stash of US Dollars which I had accumulated over two years and was planning to use to buy myself a car. They grabbed the money, got back into their car and quickly drove away.

When we reported this to the hotel and then the police they weren't surprised. They said that this was the fourth such incident that had been reported near the hotel. We felt a bit stupid that we had given over our possessions so easily but the police were adamant that we had done the right thing. They said if we had resisted in any way, the thieves would probably have just shot us.

In a taxi on the way to the airport two days later we told the taxi driver our story. He also wasn't surprised. He showed us the gun he carried on the floor between his feet and said that he had shot somebody the week before when they had tried to rob him. I was so happy to be returning to Botswana and it was a long time before I stayed too long in Jo'burg.

One time after travelling from Seronga by boat and bus I caught the bus to Gaborone and then got on a mini bus to Johannesburg. As usual I was the only white person on the bus and sat scrunched up with my pack on my knee for the eight hour journey.

I had expected to be dropped at the bus station where I knew I could call the backpackers where I usually stayed and they would pick me up. When we arrived in Jo'burg I realised that we weren't anywhere near the bus station. We were at the local kombi station. There I was – the only white person with clearly all my belongings on my back.

I had to walk up and down the line of kombis looking for one that would take me near the backpackers. The trip went without incident and even walking through a pretty seedy area from the kombi to the backpackers was okay. I realised that I had been lucky and decided that I needed to have enough money to fly in from Maun in the future.

Financial Workshops

I worked with Chillie Motshusi at Conservation International. When I decided to not renew my contract with CI and to work as a consultant I knew I would need to work with a Motswana who could translate teaching materials and help to present training programs.

Chillie was perfect. with a degree in Business Administration and experience working at grassroots level in remote areas, he was talented, experienced and had a nice patient way of dealing with people from all walks of life.

I had got a contract from the American Ambassador through USAID funding to deliver financial understanding workshops. This all had to be done within a tight time frame so once Chillie and I had written the manuals and the facilitators notes we organised a schedule.

We would travel to the first location, pitch our tents and stay overnight ready to start the next day. We had to provide all teaching materials plus food for the two days and we gave all groups a starter pack of stationery supplies and forms.

We had it down to a fine art. We would arrive back from one workshop, unload the car and have a welcome night at home. The next day we would write the workshop report and then shop for the next workshop. Then we were on our way again to the next remote location.

- The first workshop was in Gudigwa with the Bukakhwe Cultural Conservation Trust. Of course Chillie and I had both worked with this Trust before.

With the problems that they had already experienced at their own camp, it was proving difficult to attract and keep experienced

Managers and Gudigwa Camp wasn't open at the time we ran the workshop. When open, the camp provided employment for twenty people. There is little other employment in the area apart from Government projects such as the Drought Relief Programme which employed people on projects such as repairing the roads.

Gudigwa is one of the five villages in the OCT and, as such, should be guaranteed one fifth of the jobs at safari camps operating in the concession areas allocated to the OCT. Unfortunately due to labour issues only a few residents from Gudigwa were employed in the camps.

I noticed that this was a much younger Board than the one I had worked with. CI's involvement with the Gudigwa Camp project was finished and the relationship with Wilderness Safaris had become unworkable. There was now a plan to sub-lease Gudigwa Camp to take employment and management decisions away from the community. Sub-leasing would also guarantee a regular income to the community through the Board.

The ten workshop participants were all Board members and were all keen to learn. They were always punctual and focussed during the entire two days. Because of their previous financial problems they were very aware of the need for financial understanding and also of their own inexperience. They had no income to work with but it soon became clear that they would need a proper Treasurer if this project was to succeed.

- Our next workshop was with the OCT and was held at Mbiroba Camp. This was coming home for me. I knew the Board members and they knew me. I was also very aware of some of the challenges the OCT had faced. This is a very difficult Trust to administer with over six thousand people spread over five villages and numerous small settlements. Income is received from the nearby Controlled Hunting Areas leased to Okavango Wilderness Safaris to use for photographic safaris. Extensive employment in the safari camps is gained by the people in this area. Some other income comes from vehicle hire and boat transport.

The OCT had in the past attempted to provide each village with its own shop, radio station and other enterprises but had not been able to sustain this growth. They had been criticised for spending too much money on administration of the Trust.

Each village Trust Committee (VTC) had ten members – so there was a total of fifty Board members. The Executive Board consisted of ten members –two from each VTC. The Trust employed a full-time bookkeeper and a Manager.

The position of Treasurer in the VTC was a new thing. These Treasurers had not received any previous financial training and were expected to assume the responsibility for village funds but there was only one of these Treasurers participating in the workshop. The rest of the participants were mostly Chairmen or Vice Chairmen.

The workshop went well. They expressed concern that they didn't understand financial reports presented to them (usually without any real explanation) and realised that with the villages being given more financial independence there was a real need for further training. This was a successful workshop which identified their needs but only scratched the surface in providing them with the financial tools they need.

- The CgaeCgae Tlhabololo Trust is based in XaiXai. We travelled 215kms from Maun on tarred road to Nokaneng. There we turned onto a sand (and sometimes gravel) road for a further 170kms. There was only one other village on the way – Qangwa.

The most notable thing on this journey was how the colour of the sand changed. I loved the dark red sand that reminded me of the Australian outback. XaiXaiis only ten kms east of the

Botswana/Namibia border and about 10% of the population are Bombandero (Herero). The majority are Basarwa (San). There are about 500 people in the village which has a primary school and clinic.

The area of NG4 – a Controlled Hunting Area - is approximately 3000 sq kms and is described as semi-arid tree-shrub savannah. There are large sand dunes and the area is also noted for the presence of hills and caves. Together they form the Aha Aha Hills, the Gewhihaba Caves and the Komsta Hills. Rainfall is very low in this area and the soil is generally marginal. There is a lot of wildlife but it is very spread out.

XaiXai first organised themselves into a Quota Management Committee in 1995 and received the wildlife quota for the first time in 1997. The first quota was sold after the Trust was registered. Before this they had used the wildlife quota only for subsistence hunting for themselves.

Income was also received from self-drive tourists and companies offering photographic safaris. Many community members take part in dancing, story-telling and other aspects of Basarwa culture when tourists visit and this generates some income for them.

There was a borehole and piped water in some parts of the village. No electricity.

When we arrived we had to search the village to find the man with the key to open up the Trust office. Once we found him we had to wait while he washed and had tea. We were informed that most of the Board were not in the village. Five had travelled to Maun to attend a meeting in regard to a long standing problem about water holes. Another Board member was in custody after a recent murder. One woman said she was no longer interested in being on the Board, one was in Namibia and two were attending a funeral.

After consultation with the Board Vice-Secretary it was decided to invite office holders of the Village Development Committee, the Headman of XaiXai and a local policeman and teacher to participate in the workshop. It was interesting to meet a female "Headman". She was quite young and very confident.

- The Bokamoso Womens Co-Operative is located in Shorobe, 40kms from Maun on the road to the Moremi Game Reserve. This co-operative was formed in 1996 to give women an outlet for their baskets. Unfortunately once support from the NGO finished the project had foundered leaving unhappy basket producers who were owed money. The Craft Centre closed but re-opened in February 2005. A permanent shopkeeper was then employed.

The Craft Centre is ideally located to market baskets and other craft to tourists passing on their way to Moremi Game Reserve. It is a thatched building, painted bright green on the outside and there was a good sign on the road that covered all relevant information such as opening hours and contact numbers.

The Board consisted of ladies from Shorobe and surrounding areas. The Chairman was a man who had a vehicle and seemed very organised and keen to get the Co-op organised and profitable. Many of the members are older basket making ladies and do not read or write.

On the first day we had fears that this would be the first workshop to be cancelled. Despite sending a letter and then visiting Shorobe ourselves the day before to mobilise the Board members, people arrived very late. We finally got started at about 11am but we did have eleven participants by then. Some of the ladies had travelled a long way by bus to attend the training and the Chairman had returned from Maun to join us.

The group wasn't operating a bank account because they couldn't change the signatories on their original bank account until their constitution was registered. They kept a cash box in their store-room and operated out of that. Consequently the sections of the course on bank accounts, bank ledgers and monthly reconciliations didn't mean much to this group.

Ingrid Otukile from the U.S Embassy and Lovemore Sola from CI joined us as observers on the second morning of the workshop.

- The Gwezotshaa Natural Resources Trust was registered in 1995 and served three distinct communities – Gweta, Zoroga and Tshokatshee. The trust was formed on the back of a USAID funded project to process marula fruit. Unfortunately this endeavour failed and when we were there the processing machinery sat idle in the village. A water purification machine for bottling water was also in the village but not being used.

Gweta is 220kms by tarred road from Maun. It is located in Central District, right on the edge of the Makgadikgadi Pans National Park. There were two tourism operations in the area that paid a yearly fee to the Trust. There are approximately six thousand people in the village – mainly Kalanga and Basarwa.

The Makalamabedi Veterinary Gate is located 60kms from Maun and forms the border between Ngamiland and Central District. No uncooked red meat can be transported across this border to avoid the spread of foot and mouth disease.

On the day we were set to travel to Gweta Chillie turned up felling really unwell. He seemed to have a bad cold but insisted he was well enough to travel and assist with the workshops.

While I loaded the car, he sat on a chair and watched and then built himself a "nest' on the backseat where he lay and rested while I drove.

I had completely forgotten about the restrictions on transporting red meat and when we got to the gate was horrified to think we might have to leave behind the 8kgs of frozen beef that we had bought to cater for the workshop. The Police and Veterinary Officers were really sympathetic and suggested that I cook the meat. They found me a large three legged pot that I could use but I had to clean it out first. Then they generously helped me to collect some wood and light a fire.

I must admit that I am not a good fire lighter and I really struggled to keep the fire going and get the 8kg hunk of frozen meat thawed and then cooked. It was really smoky and my eyes were streaming when I looked across the road where I had parked the car to see Chillie out of the car snacking on a can of coke and a packet of biscuits. I wanted to throttle him and felt a lot less sympathy for his "man flu" after that.

It took me over an hour before the meat was cooked sufficiently. It couldn't go back into the cooler with the other food so we put it in a big bowl covered by a tea towel. We then continued on to Gweta assailed by the slightly nauseating smell of cooked meat.

Chillie again rested while I unloaded all the equipment and set up the workshop the next morning then as the workshop started he jumped up and began presenting as usual. After that he was apparently cured.

There were a lot of financial issues specific to GRNT that kept coming up. It was unfortunate that their treasurer was not there to provide some answers. We felt that this group were looking for guidance and even mediation. We didn't have access to the Deed of Trust or any past financial statements. Generally, the course content was understood and all participants contributed to discussions.

The workshops continued with our next trip to:

- Itsoseng Bomme, Shakawe Rethuseng Basket Weavers in Shakawe which is 400kms from Maun on the tarred road, right on the banks of the Okavango River. It has electricity, telecommunications and piped water. It is the main village in the area and was experiencing tremendous growth and development. The prominent ethnic group in the Shakawe area is the Hambukushu but it is the home to many tribes. It is approximately 25kms from the Namibian border and many residents of Shakawe have family ties to the Caprivi Strip area.

Itsoseng Basket Weavers' baskets are purchased by an NGO at wholesale prices. Ten percent is added to that price when they are sold to San Arts and Crafts who market overseas. The extra ten percent was returned to the weavers as a "bonus" which was deposited into the group's Post Office Account. This money could only be accessed by the weaver under special circumstances such as a death in the family or to buy school uniforms.

Xakau is on the other side of the river, reached by vehicle pontoon and then driving or walking a further 15kms on the gravel road. The village is small with no electricity and limited piped water. Most people in this village are Hambukushu. They also sell their baskets to the NGO but can't receive the 10% "bonus" because they don't have a bank account.

These groups had a very complicated system of handling money. The Chairperson and Treasurer both had authority to collect money but there were two other positions connected with the finances. These were the Bookkeeper and the Keyholder.

In theory the Book-keeper's job was to record financial transactions and the Keyholder's job was to look after the key of the cash box. In practice, the Treasurers, Bookkeepers and Keyholders were all illiterate. In any case, they didn't seem to be handling any money as this was all done through the NGO.

The Shakawe basket makers had a Craft Centre almost completed but they had no idea what was going to be involved in running the centre. They just expected that the NGO would take care of any details or problems.

We had to concentrate on the absolute basics of financial recording. Neither of these groups handled their own money and most of the women couldn't read or write. But it was really valuable for these two groups to get together to share ideas and experiences.

- The village of Nxamasere is located just off the main road – about 35kms south of Shakawe; 360kms north of Maun and is home to Nxamasere Basket Weavers and Tshwarakadiatla, Boiteko Basket Weavers. The seasonal floodplains and the Panhandle area of the Okavango Delta are very near. There are lots of elephants in the area and movement outside the village is much restricted by this, especially in the late afternoons.

There was piped water and telephones in the village and electricity was being connected.

Again baskets were sold to an NGO at wholesale prices and then sold on to San Arts and Crafts. The "bonus" scheme operates here as well.

Xhaoga is only a few kilometres from Nxamasere but the settlement is very spread out as it has developed informally from cattle posts. Because it is not a gazetted village, they couldn't be allocated a commercial plot by Land Board but this problem was eventually solved by sharing a plot with the Village Development Committee. The plot had been fenced and building work on their Craft Centre was due to start.

Samochima is only a kilometre from the Okavango River. Although the village is not gazetted they did have electricity and piped water. They sell their baskets to the NGO. The Samochima group didn't have a registered constitution so they couldn't open a Post Office Account.

Once again we had the extra positions of Book-keeper and Key Holder and they had been working with the same NGO as the other basket makers so we assumed that it was their advice to have this extra position as an extra security measure. In practice, it made the process cumbersome and discouraged people from actually using the cash boxes.

All of these groups we worked with had been established and assisted by NGOs. With some the NGOs had already moved on and the groups seemed to be drifting. I couldn't help but think that the concepts of income sharing, bonuses and money handling had come to them fully formed and didn't fit their cultures. Community members were sometimes taken too far too fast. For example, maybe the basket makers would have been happy with a stall on the side of the road and access to outside markets. Were they ready for bank accounts, fancy buildings and corporate structures?

Similarly, I thought that the clans in Gudigwa would have been better off with the development of suitable cottage industries rather that an upmarket safari camp. I understand that the camp was what the people had aspired to but, realistically, it became clear that this didn't seem to be a community that could be completely self-sufficient in running their own businesses. Sometimes things moved too quickly. I think this was true at Seronga with Mbiroba Camp as well.

Sankuyu Trust

My next project was with Sankuyu Tshwaragano Management Trust and was part of a huge review of all the Trust's activities.

Unfortunately it had been discovered that too much of the money that some Trusts were receiving was being misused or misappropriated. The Government was threatening to take management of their funds away from these Trusts and it was important to identify any weaknesses and to implement more security measures – to make Trust activities efficient and transparent.

I was contracted to conduct an operational review of this Trust. This included looking at business and administration practices in the office as well as in their tourism enterprises. The Trust was responsible for the running of Santawani Lodge and Kaziikini Campsite.

Santawani Lodge is on the edge of Moremi Game Reserve but still in the wildlife area. The Camp had six thatched huts with en-suite bathrooms. Part of my job was to inspect all aspects of the camp including the behind the scenes areas and the staff village. I then interviewed all staff members and got detailed feedback from them on their roles and the functioning of the camp and the Trust. When all of this was collated I was able to produce an Operations Manual and detailed job descriptions.

We travelled by safari vehicle through the bush from Sanatawani to Kaziikini Campsite. The trip between the camps was really enjoyable with sightings of lots of wildlife including a very obliging pride of lions that sat quietly in front of the vehicle while we enjoyed watching them rest during the heat of the day.
Kaziikini Camp was not operational at the time. I could see the potential as a cheaper stop-off for people on the way to Moremi.

There was also a traditional village opposite the campsite which provided more employment for Trust members.

At the time I was doing this work the areas of NG33 and NG34 that this Trust received income from both photographic safaris and hunting. Hunting activities have now stopped in Botswana but at the time they provided employment, income and some meat to the village of Sankuyu.

OPT Accounts

Since I had left OPT they had been helped by a South African couple who had moved to Seronga to organise the logistics for the houseboats that were now anchored in the river. I was a bit wary of this arrangement as I felt that the houseboats were taking business from the Polers Trust but I think the couples' intentions were good.

I met them on only one occasion in Seronga and shared a meal with them. I found them really critical of the Trust and its workers. They told me about how shocked they were when they had visited the Camp on Christmas Day and found the workers were making no effort to provide a Christmas meal for guests that were camping there.

I think they didn't realise that although the majority of Batswana are Christians, they didn't celebrate Christmas in the same way we do. They don't do big family meals with lots of food and expensive gifts. Christmas trees and decorations might have been seen in books but weren't part of the culture. In the same way they didn't celebrate birthdays either.

Soon after my visit the wife died suddenly and the family moved away. The Board of the OPT asked me if I would help them sort out their accounts. They arrived at my house with four black garbage bags crammed full of receipts and bits of paper that covered over two years. I spent evenings and weekends while I was employed on other projects, sorting out all the papers and then transferred everything on to spreadsheets.

I was disappointed to find that the South African "Manager" had regularly spent a lot of money on wining and dining his friends at various restaurants in Maun. Many of the receipts were for ten people for meals and drinks. He also used Trust funds to pay vet bills and buy dog food for his dogs. I can only think that he must have thought these purchases were okay as he had kept all receipts. He had spent tens of thousands of pula on non-business expenses and there was no-one to tell him he couldn't. I couldn't help contrasting this with my obsession to never use Trust money for anything that might be construed as personal expenses, resulting in me paying for a lot of things that should have been paid for by the Trust.

The Polers Trust had then approached Skill Share International and asked them to help them find a Manager. This they were able to do and it seemed to be working well for the Trust. Skill Share supplied and paid for the Manager and Trust members were able to keep earning money by poling. Business had definitely dropped off but the Camp was still open.

I also got involved helping to mediate between the Trust and a mechanic they owed money to for repairs to the Daihatsu. He ended up keeping the Daihatsu in lieu of payment but I managed to negotiate so they didn't have to pay any more money to him. Sadly I heard that they also eventually lost the truck and the motorboat because of unpaid debts. Luckily the Land cruiser was still tied to the ADF funding and couldn't be sold or seized.

I was told that a lot of polers had moved back to their villages as there wasn't enough work for them.

Time to go home

I was missing my family. It was all very well helping lots of people through my work in Botswana and I received huge satisfaction doing this work and loved the lifestyle but I now had two grandchildren and I felt it was time to go home.

The only way I got through the months until I returned home each year was by "compartmentalising" my life. When I left Sydney each year I always felt bereft and would progress through Customs and embarkation in tears. At some stage on the flight home I would put those feelings away. By the time I reached Seronga my focus was on that life.

Similarly, when I was back in Australia each Christmas, I didn't really think about Botswana.

Looking back I wonder if it was coincidence that I was always sick when I returned to Botswana each year. I was really torn about my loyalties.

I moved houses a lot when I was growing up and went to nine different Primary Schools. Then I married and moved from New Zealand to Australia. I had learnt to move on, leave old friends and old lives behind and make new ones but somehow Botswana has got into my heart. I can't hear reggae music or Bryan Adams without a strong emotional tug and a rush of memories.

Rupes was an important person in my life but I knew that we were so different. He wouldn't have fitted into my Australian life and it was time for me to leave his Botswana life.

I sold all my furniture, my car and my house and moved back to Australia.